T0383472

An Atlas of Recycled Landscapes

Michela De Poli, Guido Incerti

An Atlas of Recycled Landscapes

Cover
GTL Gnüchtel - Triebswetter
landscape architects
Old Airfield Kalbach /
Bonames
ADH [Doazan + Hirschberger
& Associés]
Jardin des Fonderies
AllesWirdGut Neugestaltung
St. Margarethen Quarry
Topotek 1
Landesgartenschau
Eberswalde
LIN
SNA Saint-Nazaire Alvéole 14
Agence Tar
Zollverein Park
Durbach Block Architects
The Brick Pit Ring

Back cover
Rosa Grena Kliass Arquitetura
Paisagística Planejamento
e Projetos Ltda
Parque da Juventude

Editor
Luca Molinari

Design
Marcello Francone

Editorial Coordination
Vincenza Russo

Editing
Valeria Perenze

Layout
Paola Ranzini

Translations
Sergio Knipe for *Scriptum*,
Rome

First published in Italy in 2014
by Skira Editore S.p.A.
Palazzo Casati Stampa,
via Torino 61
20123 Milano, Italy

www.skira.net

Printed and bound in Italy.
First edition

ISBN: 978-88-572-1079-7

Distributed in USA, Canada,
Central & South America by
Rizzoli International
Publications, Inc., 300 Park
Avenue South, New York, NY
10010, USA.
Distributed elsewhere in the
world by Thames and Hudson
Ltd., 181A High Holborn,
London WC1V 7QX, United
Kingdom.

Acknowledgments
The editors wish to thank
the many people who have
contributed to building the
chosen collection of projects
from which the present *Atlas*
has sprung, through a work of
selection. A special thanks
goes to Luca Molinari for the
patience he has shown and
for believing in the project
despite all the difficulties
that emerged, as well as
to the Skira staff who are
responsible for its publication.
Guido Incerti wishes to
dedicate this book to Eliseba,
who has always believed
in him, and to Tobia and
Simone. And to Ciro too,
a great friend—and he
knows why.
Michela De Poli wishes
to dedicate it to her
ever-evolving family.
GI, MDP

Contents

● Km²

● 50–100 ha

● 10–50 ha

• 1–10 ha

· 0–1 ha

1 Internationale Bauausstellung (IBA) Fürst-Pückler-Land (International Building Exhibition)
2 Montagna Sacra
3 Fresh Kills Park
4 Incompiuto Siciliano
5 Negev Phosphate Works
6 Redevelopment of the Unimetal Site
7 Kam Kotia KKM
8 Parc des Îles, Former Coking Plant in Drocourt
9 Pyramid
10 Tindaya Project
11 Skogskyrkogården
12 Cava Do Viriato

13 Umi-no-Mori
14 Landscape Restoration of the Vall d'en Joan Landfill Site
15 Zollverein Park
16 Adlershof Nature Reserve and Recreation Park
17 Hong Kong Wetland Park
18 Zittau-Olbersdorf Landscape Park
19 Former Saltern at La Rochelle
20 Buttes-Chaumont
21 Parque da Juventude
22 Spoor Noord Park
23 Fiumara d'Arte
24 Riemer Park
25 Natur-Park Schöneberger Südgelände

32
08 38
20 39
26 34 16 27
53 56 15 01 25
10 48 50 06 22 24 47 18

33 40 07 43 36 46

44 29 03 41 12 19 51 57 04
28 23
31 45
14 49
35 52 55
42 02
37

21

● Closed

● In progress

1 Internationale Bauausstellung
(IBA) Fürst-Pückler-Land
(International Building
Exhibition)
2 Montagna Sacra
3 Fresh Kills Park
4 Incompiuto Siciliano
5 Negev Phosphate Works
6 Redevelopment
of the Unimetal Site
7 Kam Kotia KKM
8 Parc des Îles, Former Coking
Plant in Drocourt
9 Pyramid
10 Tindaya Project
11 Skogskyrkogården
12 Cava Do Viriato

13 Umi-no-Mori
14 Landscape Restoration of the
Vall d'en Joan Landfill Site
15 Zollverein Park
16 Adlershof Nature Reserve
and Recreation Park
17 Hong Kong Wetland Park
18 Zittau-Olbersdorf
Landscape Park
19 Former Saltern at La Rochelle
20 Buttes-Chaumont
21 Parque da Juventude
22 Spoor Noord Park
23 Fiumara d'Arte
24 Riemer Park
25 Natur-Park Schöneberger
Südgelände

Foreword
Michela De Poli, Guido Incerti

This *Atlas* is the outcome of a very long process. The collecting of the material started in 2008, a year in which the need for urban recycling, the "zero consumption" of land and low-definition architecture—requirements sprung from the economic crisis whose most virulent phase began that very year—was not at that time so prominently under the eyes of everyone, scholars and the "public." The years that followed witnessed a real surge in policies, research, texts and study courses focusing on these strategies.

The present *Atlas* was established and has been developed with the aim of illustrating the desire of the human communities involved in these projects to recover their identity—possibly as a reflection of a certain "feeling of guilt" towards the landscape.

As one would expect, human society in the past always exploited the environment for its own requirements, yet without damaging it to the extent that the growth required by the industrial revolution and modernity have damaged it. Only with the latter did mankind come to shatter the balance on which rested the capacity of the natural environment to sustain human development.

At a certain point however, probably the moment in which man came to realize the uniqueness of planet Earth within the universe as a consequence of space missions,[1] did a feeling of guilt—or indeed fear—become part of global culture. Naturally, this did not lead to any substantial changes: we need only consider the failure to implement the 1995 Kyoto Protocol or the policies of adaptation that governments around the world are issuing as a response to global warming. However, this new awareness has awakened the possibility that society restore—as far as this is possible—the environments it has endangered. This represents a kind of prosthetic regeneration of the Earth's body: one possibly due to the need to re-establish the aesthetic appreciation of the landscape, and even more so a "beautiful" landscape in which to live.[2]

This, then, was point zero of our investigation. The primary point of reference in this research has been the need for the regenerated environment, for the projects presented in the *Atlas*, to provide an answer to the "wounds" which man has inflicted on certain places—as a transplant for reconstructing the image of the landscape.

The process of selection was based on the search for complex starting conditions in which the interaction between different disciplines and communities would be evident. What were sought for were not projects merely operating on empty boxes and abandoned sites in such a way as to bring about simple "changes of use," but rather projects deeply affecting the "environmental quality" as well as "social quality" of a site through its regeneration. The guiding plan and key element was provided by the wide-scale operations of territorial transformation of the IBA, where the superimposition between the history of places and the sites altered—even in terms of soil composition—is perfectly evident.

The research was not based on the components of disposal and waste, and their investigation, but was rather structured so as to illustrate the many different ways of interpreting a "recycled landscape," with the aim of documenting the vastness of the topic and its physical extension.

The choice was made, therefore, to arrange the projects in such a way that each section would include both operations spanning almost a decade and events of more limited duration. The various phases are illustrated through drawings, diagrams and photographs. For the most part, the *Atlas* features implemented projects, successfully completed recycling operations and still ongoing operations "controlled" by municipal administrations, planners and neighborhood groups, again in order to provide as broad a possible a perspective on the range of existing approaches.

All this must be seen as a partial contribution, as a first attempt to catalogue the different forces at work behind the transformation of places, to be progressively expanded through new, widespread examples of the acceptance of previously rejected landscapes.

[1] As Marshall Mc Luhan noted in the book he co-authored with Quentin Fiore: *War and Peace in the Global Village*, Bantam Books, New York 1968.
[2] Many films show environments and landscapes utterly ruined by traumatic events such as a nuclear war; few, however, explore the aesthetics of an environment damaged by over-exploitation —a far more plausible scenario.

Landscape Ready-mades
Elisa Poli

"For almost a year now, he has been taking photographs
of abandoned things"
Paul Auster, *Sunset Park*

In 1913 Marcel Duchamp presented his first *ready-made* to the public, *Roue de bicyclette*. A hundred years on, this operation still retains a subversive quality, emerging in the eyes of the viewers—including those most open to Conceptual art—as a cornerstone in the definition of 20th-century aesthetic standards. The operation was apparently a simple one: already Picasso had brought *objets trouvés* to art galleries, but unlike *ready-mades* they were added to works without ever losing their original meaning—a handlebar, while evoking the horns of a bull, still remained one of the components of a bicycle frame. Duchamp, by contrast, made a real break: it was as though his wheel—stripped of its tyre and mounted on a fork resting upside-down on a stool—was meant to be admired from the height of its pedestal as a self-sufficient and paradigmatic object. Once the wheel was removed from its frame, its formal value was transfigured, acquiring a new meaning which raised it from the status of everyday object to that of unique art piece. This change of use—a valuable practice for avant-guard currents—opened the doors to a conception of art that embraced, or indeed promoted, what were largely unexplored values at the time: selection acquired more importance than invention (for objects would be found rather than created), and what came to be regarded as "beautiful" was no longer form (since this was no longer produced by the artist) but the underlying idea. What did not change was the authorship of the artist: only when the latter presented a wheel, a bottle drainer or even a urinal as an artwork, could the public legitimately discuss its aesthetic values. The change of function of an object, action or place, therefore, had to be stated explicitly, in order for the poetics of *transformation* to be treated on an equal footing as that of *creation* in the 20th century.

This factor, which may have been enough for art a century ago, would not appear to have proven as popular in the architectural sphere in the same period: for the latter, the appeal of the *new = beautiful* equation limited—at any rate within the official culture or that en vogue—any regionalist tendency, any (apparent) link with the past or what was already in existence. The dogmas formulated by Le Corbusier—first breached in the 1930s—haunted the minds of whole generations of planners, who did their best to turn reinforced concrete into a founding myth and the flat roof into a universally applicable rule. The model of the "modern house"—recently represented in the French Pavilion at the 14th Venice Architecture Biennale and beautifully illustrated in Jaques Tati's film *Mon oncle*—called for the surgical demolition of pre-existing structures (the Paris of the Marais and Canal Saint-Martin) and the construction of futuristic *machines à habiter*, of which the French director made a most amusing parody. Without wishing to oversimplify or dismiss the complex and fascinating reasons that led to the formulation of the myth of modernity in the architectural sphere, it is useful to recall how, to this day, the production of environmental landmarks is almost entirely based on planning from scratch. In a society marked by precariousness, in which social media as much as the economy and politics encourage the frantic replacement of images and narratives, the presence of large architectural works conceived as ever-lasting and featuring cutting-edge technology provides reassurance to a public in search of points of reference.

What is immediately visible—however difficult it may be to understand, given the complexity of many large projects executed in the past twenty years—and what may be evaluated according to the paradigm of innovation (an interesting version of the *new* = *beautiful* equation en vogue in the 1920s) would not appear to require any lengthy analysis: the positivist faith in a science capable of building its own temples and thus of governing Nature is a recurrent cultural feature difficult to deconstruct. Perhaps this is why the extensive research and selection work carried out by Guido Incerti and Michela De Poli proves so useful: because what it offers is an *Atlas*, a tool for simplification—but certainly not over-simplification—which helps the reader access a different world, albeit one far more frequented today than one would imagine. The *Atlas* carries the weight of an extremely rich, high-quality international itinerary, in which the scale of each project conforms to particular and often fragile requirements—the marker of a reality far more uneven and composite than what the slick image of the "archistar" model has to offer. The poetics of ready-made merge with a detailed knowledge of the requirements of areas that are underestimated precisely because they are all too often examined with a view merely to formal profit, to an immediate, poorly structured return on image. Recycled landscapes are instead designed to erase the fate which all too often springs from a forgotten past and a denied future: in the planned present many places are regenerated and transformed in terms of their use and meaning rather than their form, in such a way as to acquire a new significance, a renewed experiential value. The fifty-seven projects illustrated in this volume are interesting devices to be conceptually explored and read as maps of rediscovered and regenerated area. They provide an exhaustive selection for anyone wishing to train their gaze to develop a more conscious interpretation of man-made environments.

The value of the projects lies in the leisurely reflection they afford, in metamorphosis as a symbol of continuity, and—most importantly—in a human imprint which does not impose anything new but rather discloses what is already there: proof of how excellent results can be achieved even without imposing any hyper-authorship on places. The quality of the planning is evident from the fact that the projects presented in this book have the great merit of highlighting faded outlines, changing the public's view through a range of expedients that often come across as the techniques for architectural *ready-mades*. The approach based on exploration that is predominant here stands in contrast to the kind of conquering approach suggested by the swarms of cranes scattered across the suburbs. Existing areas are already replete with structures, and the many planners in this book have been very good at grasping and representing them through compelling narratives. Herein lies the value of the present *Atlas* which, despite the terse rigor of its presentation of different examples, discloses stories as long as novels.

Km²

Designing New Landscapes
Rolf Kuhn

The need to be proactive in dealing with countryside exploited by mining is an understanding which has spread throughout the world and has already left its mark in many places. It is no longer acceptable in the 21st century for people to abdicate their responsibility for the future. And there is a willingness to create new landscapes and a need to rebalance social, economic and ecological concerns. Indeed, a diverse, multifunctional landscape infrastructure is the only means of providing the solid basis required for the local economy and the best prospects for the local people. Therefore a sustained process of redevelopment is also an investment in the future which generates added value. Lusatia in the east of Germany is leading by example in this regard.

Since industrialization, its landscape has been ravaged so severely that nature's self-healing powers are exhausted. How can it go on? Can the destruction of nature and the demolition of entire villages be "put right" by filling in and reclaiming huge open-cast mine pits and turning them into farmland, forest and building land, by transforming any remaining cavities into bodies of water, by laying waste old industrial estates to make way for new developments and fallow land, and by removing all traces of the industrial past? Is that the way to make amends? Or should nature simply be left to recover by itself without any intervention and redevelopment work? As soon as the diggers stop and the pumps are switched off, the groundwater would rise again and new lakes would emerge within a matter of decades—but these lakes would be acidic. Without human intervention nature would gradually reconquer the region bit by bit and the result would be a unique natural landscape, but this is a scenario which harbors many risks and which would make vast expanses of Lusatia no-go areas that would be of no practical use to humans and would be uninhabitable for a hundred years.

This is why it is better for man to intervene and redevelop the land, reinforcing shore areas, flooding pits and neutralizing the waters, clearing areas to allow nature to return, and creating new usable areas. But it would not be right for man to "wipe away" all traces of Lusatia's industrial past in the redevelopment process, but rather to retain outstanding examples of architecture and landscape which attest to the mixed blessing of the region's industrial history. After all, it is these eyewitnesses that characterize the region, is it not? And is it not also true that dismantling and conventional regeneration measures only serve to rob people of their identity, history and life histories? For this reason the aim of the Internationale Bauausstellung Fürst-Pückler-Land was to preserve particularly impressive examples of Lusatia's industrial heritage and to integrate them in-

to a new development path for Lusatia, and it has advocated this cause with its partners in a ten-years lasting process. The most famous example is the F60 visitor mine in Lichterfeld. The F60 and its neighbor, the emerging Lake Bergheid, are symbolic of the IBA strategy in that the old rubs shoulders with the new, regional identity is preserved, and new things are born out of wild imaginings and great creativity, thus providing the driving force and inspiration for sustainable regional development. Hence the strategy for the development of the Lusatian Lakeland and the vision for a variety of characteristic designs for thirty man-made lakes in a sparsely populated region. Hence the traditional engineering spirit of the region is now rising to new challenges and is needed to create a varied and exciting new landscape, which will offer quality of life and will be able to compete in the race to attract creative minds, investors and tourists. At the end of the 1990s it was decided to provide support for the lignite mine redevelopment process by bringing in an International Building Exhibition to provide vision and creative input and to set the wheels of change in motion in a region exploited for its riches and left depleted.

Internationale Bauausstellung (IBA)
Fürst-Pückler-Land (International Building Exhibition)

Location:
Lusatia, Brandenburg, Germany
Plan: 2000–10
Implementation: 2010
Ordering party:
Region Lausitz-Spreewald
Project team:
IBA Fürst-Pückler-Land GmbH, about 20 employees
Collaborators:
Mining companies, communities and towns, companies, associations, private partners, planning offices, universities
Previous use:
Pit/lignite deposit
Current use: Public park
Surface:
7000 km² (1.7 million acres)

For ten years the Internationale Bauausstellung (IBA) Fürst-Pückler-Land organization has been active in shaping the post-mining landscape in Brandenburg (Eastern Germany). This region was known as the energy district of the former German Democratic Republic because of its huge deposits of lignite. Initially, mining activity was below ground but it was later moved onto the surface, in huge opencast mines. Mining favored the development of other industries such as briquette factories, power stations, coke plants and related branches of industry. Subsequent to the radical political change in 1989–90, the majority of the opencast mines and industries were abruptly shut down. Today, five opencast mines and three power stations are operating in the region.

As a result of this deindustrialization process, the region has experienced a high rate of unemployment. The redevelopment of former mines, industrial sites and brownfields has been a challenging task. Against this background, the government has allocated special funds for regeneration and has established a state company, LMBV (Lausitzer und Mitteldeutsche Bergbau-Verwaltungsgesellschaft). In a parallel step, the Region initiated an international building exhibition, Internationale Bauausstellung (IBA) Fürst-Pückler-Land 2000–10, to accompany the process of reclamation and open up new perspectives for regional development.

IBA Fürst-Pückler-Land has been engaged in a total of thirty projects with seven main topics:

- industrial heritage: the aim of IBA is not only to preserve outstanding examples of Lusatian industrial heritage, but also to invent new possible uses for those sites. The different locations are connected by the Energy Route of Lusatian Industrial Heritage, thus creating a unique touristic experience;
- waterscapes: the new aquatic design is one main aspect of the post-mining landscape. The coal pits that have fallen into disuse—around thirty in the whole region—were flooded to become lakes. The "heart" of the new Lusatian Lakeland is a chain of ten lakes that are connected by navigable canals. Apart from the recreation and sports opportunities, floating houses became a new hallmark of the Lusatian Lakeland;
- energy landscapes: the extensive, sparsely populated region provides ideal preconditions for electricity production from regenerative energy sources like wind, sun and biomass. We have been examining concepts for energy landscapes to combine different energy sources for a new, variably usable and ecologically enduring cultural landscape;
- new land: opencast mining allows one to shape newly filled-in landscapes with a new contour and new uses. We have developed several different approaches for post-mining landscapes to give them a characteristic design—landscapes that do not represent a denial of mining and give the region outstanding examples of landscape architecture;
- border landscapes: development along the border of two nations always represented a particular challenge, especially along the German-Polish border. The drawing of the border following the Second World War separated cultural landscapes and towns that formerly belonged together. With Poland's entry into the European Union, new opportunities for cross-border cooperation have opened up;
- cityscapes: a huge decrease in population has resulted from the deindustrialization of the region. In particular, this affects the towns that had previously grown because of the industrialization and now, in turn, are shrinking.

IBA has been accompanying the conversion of towns and demonstrating new approaches to demolition and the re-valuing of spaces;
- transitional landscapes: opencast mining results in desert- and canyon-like interim landscapes, which radiate a bizarre beauty. Through opencast mining tours, IBA makes it possible to experience these landscapes, enabling visitors to discover new beauties in a landscape that has fundamentally changed and to open their minds to new developments.
Based on IBA's experiences, we have formulated ten principles concerning the treatment of post-mining landscapes. In 2010, IBA had its final presentation, but the projects and ideas will live on and will be further developed.

Montagna Sacra

Location:
Cilento and Vallo di Diano
National Park, Italy
Plan: 1998
Implementation: 2000
Ordering party:
Ente PNCVD, Comunità
Montana Alento - Monte
Stella, Lagambiente
Campania and the local
municipalities (agreement
for the development
of the project)
Project team:
*Planning and coordination
during implementation:*
Architect Giuseppe Anzani
Collaborators:
Music: Antonello Paliotti;
synchronic arrangement
Nicola Polito; *logistics
and operating of the bells:*
Associazione Montanari-
Ripe Rosse
Previous use:
Mountain villages
Current use: Soundscape
Surface:
100 km² (24,710 acres)
Cost: 25,000 euros

The sound installation *Montagna Sacra* seeks to promote a specific landscape
through the recovery and reinterpretation of one of its defining features.
A description of the context—of which the project is ultimately just a temporary
extension—is crucial to justify the choices that have been made, and in a way
even to defend the "need" for them.
Mount Stella is a 1130-meter-high mountain located between the Alento River
and the Tyrrhenian Sea. Its regular conical outline stands out against the sea
and is visible across most of Cilento, in the southern tip of the province
of Salerno. At the foot of the mountain, thirty small villages form a network
covering a total distance of up to 6 kilometers, with only a very small distance
(no more than 1 or 2 kilometers) between one village and the next.
The geomorphology and history of this area have made it a markedly collective
and polycentric environment, and this is reflected by many local traditions,
on a small and wide scale. Some of these traditions are truly unique,
as in the case of a ceremony that takes place on the landscape scale when
on Good Friday the confraternities of each village go on a simultaneous pilgrimage
to the other centers. This engenders a real web of ritual "visits" that sets
hundreds of inhabitants in motion all at the same time across the slopes
of Mount Stella (a far from negligible demographic sample, given a population
of a few thousand residents).
On account of the marked proximity of the villages, each of which—however
small—has its own parish church, the mountain has a very high density of bell
towers: one of the highest (if not the highest) in contemporary rural Europe.
The bell tower marks the center of the village and represents it within the visual
landscape of the countryside. Likewise, the sound of its bells represents the
village within the soundscape, both because of its physical extension—it was
among the loudest man-made sounds in the pre-industrial era—and because
of its semantic significance among populations that resort to it to get their
bearings within the "circular" time of working or festive days, as well as to gain
crucial information on unexpected occurrences (accidents, disasters, etc.).
Given that the distribution of bell towers creates an unbroken belt
of superimposed sound fields skirting the whole perimeter of the mountain,
so that in several locations it is possible to hear even sub-systems of five or more,
a "concert" has been developed for the sixty bells of the thirty local bell towers.
The music has been composed by taking into account the unique sound features
of each bell tower: in particular, the pitch and intensity of its sounds; the mode
of percussion (with short swifts strokes and/or by pealing out); the mode
of operation or control (manual, electromechanical or digital). The composition
also takes account of the orography and of the proximity of the bell towers,
and is meant to be listened to from some specific locations that have been
chosen on account of their central position with respect to the sub-systems
identified. The installation thus makes the most of existing bell towers, without
altering their structure in any way and exclusively resorting to traditional modes
of execution. This has ensured the active participation and support
of the inhabitants of the villages.

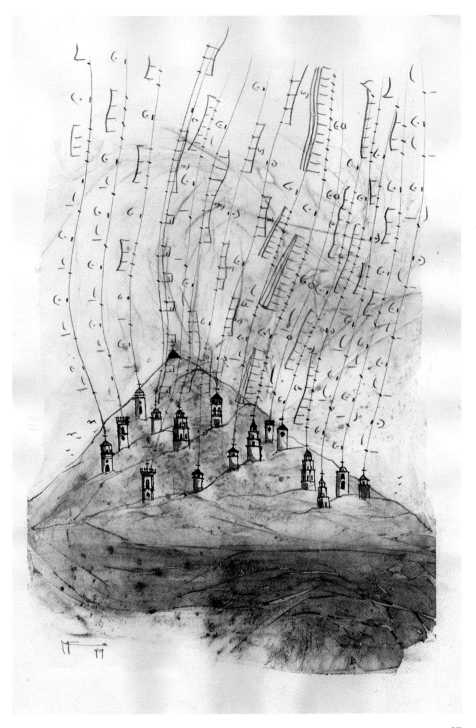

Fresh Kills Park

Location:
Staten Island, New York
Plan: 2002
Implementation: 2010–40
Ordering party:
City of New York Parks
& Recreation
Project team:
James Corner Field
Operations, HR&A, HDR,
Rogers Surveying,
Geosyntec, Langan
Engineering, Halcrow
Yolles, Biohabitats, Applied
Ecological Services, AKRF,
Philip Habib & Associates,
Project Projects,
Mierle Ukeles Artist,
Faithful & Gould
Previous use: Landfill site
Current use: Public park
Surface:
8.9 km² (2,200 acres)
Cost: 1.5 million euros

Between the years of 1948 and 2001, the City of New York produced enough garbage to make Fresh Kills the largest landfill in the world. Since its closure in 2001, the value and meaning of this 9-square-kilometer urban site has changed entirely. This artificial landscape, located on the western edge of Staten Island, is now viewed as an extraordinary asset to the growing metropolitan population with increasing and urgent needs for open space.

Only 45% of Fresh Kills is actual landfill. The rest of the site remains true to the original landscape of wetlands native to the New York archipelago. The result is an unusual and striking combination of gigantic tightly capped and managed grassy mounds dominating large expanses of flat forested wetlands and creeks. The great variety of natural settings resulting from this highly unusual landscape provides extraordinary habitats for multitude of local or migratory wildlife.

Field Operations' vision is to transform Fresh Kills into a 21st-century urban park that will maintain both its big scale and elemental character while carefully restoring its native landscapes. Sustainable design strategies are integrated into the design process and revealed to the public. Buildings and activities are concentrated in specific areas leaving the rest of the site as open and natural as possible. Because of its extreme size and topography, Fresh Kills Park lends itself to both recreational and scenic uses. It naturally divides into five areas, North Park, East Park, South Park, West Park and the Confluence. In order to ensure a coherent design strategy for the whole, while maintaining the unique characteristics of the parts, the Fresh Kills Park Master Plan provides a framework based on ecological processes that will recover not only the health and biodiversity of ecosystems, but also the spirit and imagination of people who will visit this extraordinary place. The construction of such a large park in an urban context presents many complex technical, administrative and political challenges. The project is phased over a thirty-year period, with a compelling and achievable first phase within the first ten years. Sections of North Park and South Park are a part of this first phase.

The implementation strategy proposes a series of flexible and incremental stages that will ensure a working balance between landfill closure, processes of site management and the transformation of the site into an urban public park.

The 94-hectare North Park overlooks a wildlife refuge. It is programmed primarily for wildlife and passive recreation. It will include multiuse pathways, scenic overlooks, picnic areas, and an observation platform overlooking the creeks and refuge. The project also includes a seed farm which will be used to grow the seed used to plant other areas of Fresh Kills Park in future phases.

The 172-hectare South Park is deeply nestled in the heart of Fresh Kills Park. It includes two distinct capped mounds as well as extensive areas of tidal and freshwater wetlands and forests linking to adjacent parks. Extremely varied natural settings lend themselves to a variety of public uses, including simply experiencing the site from multiple vantage points. A 4-kilometre multi-use path is planned to allow visitors to walk, run and cycle through this landscape. The journey will highlight the great variety of ecological habitats and landscape experiences, while leading visitors from lowland areas to hilltops where they can enjoy panoramic views of the park, the meandering creeks and the Staten Island context beyond.

In sum, this is a very long term project, which deploys a time-based approach to regenerating damaged sites and designing them for new social and ecological functions.

HABITAT PHASING 7/20/94 DRAFT

| existing habitats | phase 1 | phase 2 | phase 3 | phase 4 | mature biomatrix |

GRASSLAND
STRIP CROPPING

Strip cropping is an inexpensive, industrial scale technique for increasing the organic content of poor soils, chelating metals and toxins (inhibiting their uptake by plants), increasing soil depth, controlling weeds and increasing aeration.

A crop rotation system is proposed to improve the existing topsoil cover without importing large quantities of new soil.

The cultivated soils will support native prairie and meadow. In the wetter areas of the mounds, shallow-rooted successional woodland will ultimately diversify the grassland biotopes.

NORTH AND SOUTH MOUNDS west face 130 acres
NORTH AND SOUTH MOUNDS east face 95 acres
EAST AND WEST MOUNDS east face 220 acres
EAST AND WEST MOUNDS west face 250 acres

WOODLAND
ON THE MOUNDS

2 to 3 feet of new soil will be required for cultivation of denser, stratified woodland on the mounds in early stages of the park's development. The new soils would be stabilized and planted with native grassland initially to create a weed-resistant matrix for the gradual interplanting of young tree stock.

Proposed woodland on the mounds is located in areas adjacent to proposed lowland and swamp forests to widen the habitat corridor while conserving the amount of new soil to be imported.

A total of 220 acres of woodland on the mounds is proposed—with 65 acres on the north and south mounds, and 155 acres on the east and west mounds.

NORTH AND SOUTH MOUNDS 65 acres
EAST AND WEST MOUNDS 155 acres

LOWLAND FOREST

When a supply of native saplings and tree plugs are available (particularly in early years of park construction when other areas are being prepared for planting), lowland and swamp forests are planted in overlapping ecotonal bands on existing soil to build the woodland rim.

EXPRESSWAY CORRIDOR + NORTH AND SOUTH MOUNDS 160 acres
EAST AND WEST MOUNDS

YEAR 1 2 3 4 5 6 7 8 9 10 11 12 13 14 15 16 17 18 19 20 21 22 23 24 25 26 27 28 29 30 31 32 33 34 35 36 37 38 39 40

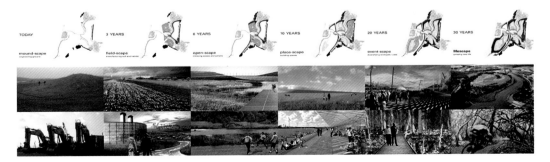

| TODAY | 3 YEARS | 6 YEARS | 10 YEARS | 20 YEARS | 30 YEARS |
| mound-scape | field-scape | open-scape | place-scape | event-scape | lifescape |

Incompiuto Siciliano

Location:
Giarre (Catania), Italy
Plan: 2006
Implementation
in progress
Ordering party:
Fondazione Incompiuto
Siciliano
Project team:
Alterazioni Video
(Paololuca Barbieri Marchi,
Andrea Masu, Alberto
Caffarelli, Giacomo Porfiri,
Matteo Erenbourg, Enrico
Sgarbi, and Claudia D'Aita)
Collaborators:
Iole Bianchi, Alessandro
Boscarino, Vanni Brusadin,
Nicola Danese, Fabrizio
Giardina Papa, Veronica
Locatelli, Giulia Lambiase,
and Giancarlo Zammù
Previous use: Various
Current use:
Archaeological park
of unfinished architecture
Surface:
3 km² (741 acres)

San Giacomo dei Capri
bridge, Naples

Distribution
of unfinished works

Incompiuto Siciliano is an Italian landscape project which explores the phenomenon of unfinished public works. The project seeks to reverse the negative perception of these architectural structures by raising them to the rank of artworks and thus turning them into an economic resource. The aim of Incompiuto is not to deliver any political or social exposé, but rather to make the point that these new ruins of contemporary architecture are sites of a collective memory yet to be explored— that unfinished works are artworks. To support this bold claim to artistry, the project has been structured into three stages of development. The first stage consists in the conceptual planning of the whole operation through the creation of an annotated catalogue and map of unfinished architectural works, illustrating the phenomenon from an iconographic, processual and historical perspective. The analysis of the data obtained by this means has led to the publication of a "Manifesto1," identifying the distinctive features of what we have chosen åto term the "Unfinished architectural style." This "style" has proved to be not so much a mere label applicable to a heterogeneous group of works, as a theoretical model and interpretative paradigm for identifying and foreseeing the configuration of unfinished works or systems of works.

The second stage in the project is a working stage based on the planning and establishment of the first Archaeological Park of Unfinished Architecture. The ideal location for the Park is in the municipality of Giarre in the province of Catania. This town, voted the capital of Sicilian Unfinished Architecture because of the density of unfinished buildings it boasts, may be regarded as the epicenter for the development of this style. As such, it represents a unique setting in which to develop new ideas, new professional skills and new economic enterprises. With the idea of an archaeological Park of Sicilian Unfinished Architecture—a way of boosting the economic sector of cultural tourism—for the first time unfinished works come to constitute a resource, meeting a goal on which the future of the whole project depends. While the cataloguing and mapping of unfinished architecture and the subsequent establishment of the Park represent two important stages of development in the project, the third and last stage consists in envisioning future scenarios for all unfinished works in Italy. This transition is so crucial that it marks the passage from a negative phase of denunciation to a positive phase of suggestions, in which—once the problem has been acknowledged—new modes of intervention are planned. This third, "concrete" stage coincides with the celebration of the work in the Italian Pavilion of the 2010 Venice Architecture Biennale. Under these auspices,[1] Incompiuto leaves the field of art to merge with that of architecture. Yet while this acknowledgement on the part of the public may no doubt be deemed a celebration, one can only hope that it is not a funeral celebration. For it is quite evident that only four logistic options may be envisaged with regard to the fate of the vast national heritage constituted by unfinished buildings: completion, demolition, reuse and establishment as a memorial museum. Should Incompiuto Siciliano be dismissed as only the latest futile exposé, the risk will be that of yielding to a collective hypnosis. If, conversely, the project is well received by the authorities, by planners and by construction companies as a chance to make up for an opportunity for progress previously missed, and if the challenge to make a museum of this collective failure is taken up, then Incompiuto Siciliano may well signal a bold awakening.

[1] *Abitare*, no. 486, October 2008.

Playground in the
Incompiuto Siciliano
Archaeological Park of
Giarre (CT), Italy

San Giacomo dei Capri
bridge, Naples

The Negev Phosphate Works

Location:
North Yorkeam mining field,
Negev desert, Israel
Plan: 1990
Implementation:
1990–present
Ordering party:
Negev Phosphate Works
Project Team:
Shlomo Aronson,
Eitan Eden, Yair Avigdor,
Ami Gvirtzman
Collaborators:
Yair Levi (Chief geologist)
Previous use: Mine
Current use:
Morphological riqualification
Surface:
2.5 km² (643 acres)

The Negev Phosphate Works is one of Israel's major mining industries.
For decades, Negev phosphates have been removed through opencast mining.
The result was the creation of a desolate landscape of quarries with adjacent
waste heaps some 40 meters high.
Mounting pressure from the "Greens," the Natural Reserve Authority,
and an increasing public awareness of the effects of opencast mining, compelled
the company to commission a plan to deal with the ecological and environmental
damage caused by its mines.
The mining company demanded that the solution not be prohibitively costly,
and should be technically practical. The size of the site was about 256 hectares,
and it is part of the basin of one of the largest *wadis* in the Israeli desert,
the 120-kilometer-long Zin Valley. It included phosphates of different qualities
(low organic, high organic, and bituminous). The phosphate was usually found under
a layer of approximately 16 meters of alluvial or conglomerate material and 8 meters
of clay. The most striking and visible geo-morphological element in the vicinity
of the site was a natural system of crescent-shaped "hogbacks."
The common mining practice is simply an efficient response to the economic
and technical constraints. The results on a landscape are usually devastating.
Huge quarry pits are filled with very high mounds of dumped material. The steep
angle of repose, the repetitive engineering morphology, and the scale of the
dumping are all foreign, by definition, to the environment. The typical rehabilitation
effort to smooth and cover the damage is frequently not sufficient since it is not
part of a comprehensive topographical design strategy for that location.
The new mining procedure which was proposed and was successfully
implemented had four elements. First, preservation: the *wadi* which ran through
the center of the site was to be preserved; this preservation would also help

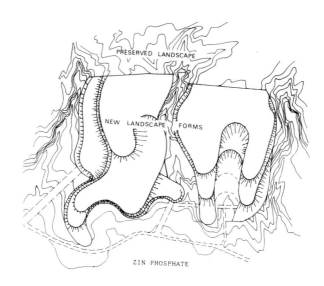

reduce the huge scale of the earthworks. The second issue was containment: a special effort was made to confine surface damage *only* to the area where the phosphate was actually mined. In order to do this, a plan was made showing what had to be mined and what had to be dumped in each stage. Mining and dumping areas alternated, like a giant *Musical Chairs*, with the progress of the work. With the exception of the first 3 million tons, all the moving earth was confined within the mine itself, and was not allowed on, or outside, the excavation borders, contrary to past practice. This procedure had to take into account the different quality of the phosphate layers, the technological constraints on the movement of the huge trucks, and the economic demands for efficiency. The creation of a new morphology was the third element in the plan. The area of the mine, plus the area of the first 3 million tons of fill which had to be dumped on the edge of the site (out of 40 million for the whole operation) had to be given a shape. An important idea was to relate to the typical natural forms of the site, so that when the mining was complete, the landscape would still resonate as authentic. Out of many possibilities, the solution chosen related to the image of the crescent-shaped hogbacks. These natural formations, common in the area, were the right shape and height in the original landscape to accommodate the amount of material which had to be repositioned.

Lastly, the scale of the sculpted tailings deposit had to fit into the existing landscape. In order to reduce the gigantic scale of the dumping, the mounds were divided into steps of 10 meters with a setback, instead of the previous practice of creating 30- to 40-meter steps. The end result was that a new landscape in the Zin region of the Negev was created with self-referential scaling and the use of forms which were fitting to that particular place, at the cost of only two cents extra per ton.

Redevelopment of the Unimetal Site

Location:
District of Greater Caen,
banks of the Orne River,
Normandy, France
Plan:
1994 (competition, winning
project); 1994–97 (urban
development scheme)
Ordering party:
District of Greater Caen
Project team:
Dominique Perrault
Architecture
Collaborators:
Erik Jacobsen (agronomist
engineer, hydrogeologist)
Previous use:
Iron and steel industrial site
Current use: Public park
Surface:
2.5 km² (618 acres)

The work at Caen is related to the dismantling of an industrial plant, a large steel mill covering a vast area. Mining used to provide support for the whole city and the dismantling of the mining site left a black hole, not just in economic terms, but also for the social life, landscape and urban organization of the area. The site is located within a plain surrounded by hills that bear the traces of the old infrastructures of the SMN (Société Métallurgique de Normadie). These trace the lines connecting the countryside to the urban fabric.
The project consists in the recomposition and development not of one but of several landscapes.
Its defining qualities are those of a pre-landscape operation linking nature and architecture.
The project was developed by setting a geometrical grid (100 x 100 meters) on the bare land where the steel mill used to be located, with the aim of marking out an area whose new identity was still uncertain, thereby encouraging new forms of reappropriation.
The essential features of the site were then drawn: at the head of the valley, an old road cutting across the plant was connected to nearby areas through a large-scale plan that brings together a range of different activities and—most importantly—fosters new modes of engagement with nature.
The rigidity of the regular grid is altered by the variety of wild and rural landscapes it can enclose.

Kam Kotia KKM

Location:
Robb Township, Ontario,
Canada
Plan: 2000
Implementation: 2012–50
Ordering party:
Abandoned Mines
Rehabilitation Program
(AMRP)
Project team:
The Rehabilitation
Inspection and Compliance
Section of the Ministry
of Northern Development,
Mines and Forestry
(MNDMF); Ministry of
Natural Resources (MNR),
and the Ministry of
Environment (MOE);
Project coordinator:
Chris Hamblin
Collaborators:
Ontario Mining Association
(OMA)
Previous use: Mine
Current use: Public park
Surface: 2 km² (494 acres)
Cost: 62 million dollars
(total cost of all
rehabilitation)

The Kam Kotia Mine site (KKM) is located in Robb Township, which is about 35 kilometers northwest of the municipality of Timmins, Ontario, Canada. The KKM copper/zinc ore body was discovered in the late 1920s. However, no mining occurred on the site until 1942 when the Canadian Wartime Metals Corporation rushed the site into production for its war materials. The site operated for approximately two years from an open pit, closing in 1944. The tailings produced at this time were simply allowed to flow out into the surrounding lands. The KKM site went back into production in 1961 and was operated by a private mining company until 1972. By the end of the mine's life, approximately 6 million tons of highly sulphidic ore had been milled at the site. Most of the ore was from the KKM site, but sulphide-rich ore from the neighboring Jameland Mine was also milled at KKM. The tailings were released into the environment to both the south and the north of KKM flowing out over vast areas. Finally, in the late 1960s, rudimentary impoundment dams were constructed in the northwest area of the site, to allow tailings closest to the mill to be stacked to a higher elevation. Unfortunately these dams did not contain or control any of the acidic, metal leachate-bearing drainage that resulted over the next several decades.

In the late 1970s, the owners offered to surrender the KKM site back to the Crown. As acid mine drainage (or AMD) was not understood at that time, the surrender was allowed and the ownership of the site returned to the Crown. Several years later the company that had operated the site went into bankruptcy. Over time, the KKM AMD killed all aquatic flora and fauna in both the Little Kamiskotia River to the south of the site and the Kamiskotia River to the north and east of the site. There were also concerns that the AMD would pollute groundwater coming from the site, which could impact on the local residents. These concerns resulted in a written complaint being made by local residents to the Environmental Commissioner of Ontario. In order to address this concern, and recognizing the priority of the KKM site, Ontario decided to fund the rehabilitation of the KKM site.

A conceptual rehabilitation plan was developed for MNDMF in the year 2000. The rehabilitation measures laid out in this plan were the result of a consortium of consulting firms reviewing all possible rehabilitation measures and then determining the best possible solution for the site. The goal of the rehabilitation measures is to reduce the size of the footprint of the site, seal the remaining tailings areas so that oxidation of the tailings and AMD production ceases, and the surrounding environment, including both the lands and waters, return to its original pre-mining state.

The conceptual rehabilitation plan predicts that it will take approximately three full flushings of groundwater to remove all remaining contaminants from the drainage exiting the site. The KKM water treatment plant will need to continue to operate for this entire period of time, which the consultants predict will take fifty years or more.

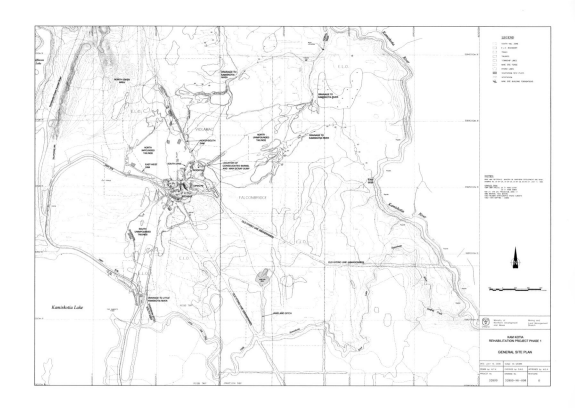

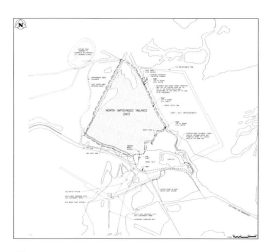

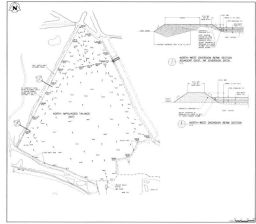

44

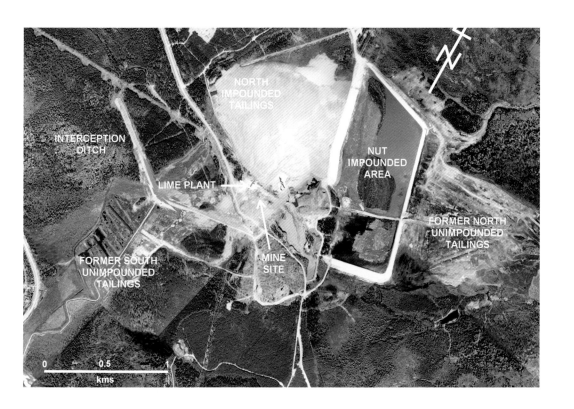

Parc des Îles, Former Coking Plant in Drocourt

Location: Drocourt, Rouvroy, Henin-Beaumont, France
Plan: 2005 (competition)
Implementation: 2005–09 first phase; 2012–13 second phase
Ordering party: Communauté d'Agglomération d'Hénin-Carvin
Project team: *Landscape, urban planning:* Ilex (team leader), Sylvie Duval (landscapist, HQE [High Environmental Quality] consultant); *infrastructure and economic management:* Maning; *environmental technologies:* Tauw
Previous use: Coal-processing site
Current use: Public park
Surface: 1.6 km^2 (395 acres) – first stage: 45 ha
Cost: 6.6 million euros

After the demolition of the plants, the 395 acres (160 hectares) of the coking plant were brought back to their purest form: a vast flatland surmounted by three black slag heaps.
The project is conceived as an urban development strategy in which the landscape becomes a tool for renewal and for densification. It is necessary to reconstruct the margins of the park, to densify and connect towns, and to use the free space to design a "nature city."
The various functions—economic (free zone), residential (Europan 8, 2005) and leisure (ponds and refined gardens designed by artists)—interconnect and overlap with one another around a showcase space, a sort of lively public "yard," south of the urban area.
The "mound park" by far exceeds the purpose for which it was designed, as well as the leisure and green functions it was initially assigned, by affecting the process of definition of the urban landscape.
The first operational phase has reshaped a new geography, with some 200,000 cubic meters of cut and fill operations on site. The excavations have created a 17-acre (7-hectare) lake with "theme" islands: a real jewel in the park's crown that finds a counterpart in the wooded areas and "dry" islands overlooking the large meadow.
A new foundation for the future, multi-purpose and capable of accommodating numerous leisure, educational or nature-related activities.

BILLY-MONTIGNY

HENIN-BEAUMONT

terril

terril 205

ROUVROY

île d'accueil
du grand parc

le parc des îles
1ère phase
en cours de réalisation

ZA Picasso

DROCOURT

ZA Chênaie

Pyramid

Location:
Arsuf Kedem, Israel
Plan: 2008
Implementation: 2009–10
Ordering party:
Green Gallery
Project team:
Daniel Manheim,
Tanya Preminger
Collaborators: Park Dina
Previous use:
Dismissed area, landfill site
Current use:
Public park for Nature Art
Surface:
1.4 km² (350 acres)

An area of 350 acres around Arsuf Kedem, Israel, on the shores of the Mediterranean Sea, between ancient city ruins and a modern village, was declared a nature reserve in 2003.

The area was not fenced off and the access remained unlimited for a long time, so in fact it became a no-man's land—a place where contractors dump their construction trash, concrete boards, blocks and metal leftovers and plastic bags, making the area unpleasant and unusable for visitors.

Park Dina, an ecological garden which is situated next to the dump, managed by Mr. Daniel Manheim, and the Green Gallery, curated by Mrs. Tanya Preminger, undertook a mission to clean up the area and turn it back to the public. They made it a goal to re-cycle the landscape, to re-plant the natural vegetation of the site and expand the clean areas where Nature Art would be displayed. The visitors of the park will be able to take pleasure in its natural landscape and fresh air, and on top of that get spiritual oxygen—enjoy art made from nature and about nature.

Most of the construction trash scattered in the area was situated next to the road, so the first steps in the recycling plan were to create a few large scale earth works by the side of the road to hide the trash in.

In the course of the work a bulldozer owned by the Green Gallery was piling up the construction trash and concrete boards, clearing up an area of around 10,000 square meters. The huge pile was covered in natural soil and sculptured by Tanya Preminger's hands to create the *Pyramid* sculpture.

The sculpture consists of four large udders pointing upwards—the answer to the gift of life granted us by the supreme creator. These four piles of earth are images of a temple, an altar, a cradle, and the firmament of heaven. They all originate from the large belly of the creator, Mother Nature.

Earth as a material used in art arouses powerful feelings. In most people's minds earth connects to home, homeland, motherhood, creation, birth and nurture.

The biggest pile of trash was made into the *View Point* sculpture. The trash was covered with earth and sculptured to form a huge crescent. It is the largest and highest mass in the area and serves as a focal point and as a view point, since a path was created along the crescent, and viewers can climb up.

Its highest point can serve as a stage as well, as happened in the opening of the exhibition, when a band of musicians played the trumpets and trombone from the summit.

The natural vegetation of the Mediterranean seashore was planted back around the sculpture.

Work in the park is far from over. There are plenty more piles of trash around, and on the other hand many holes in the soil, where contractors took the sand away. While the work is still in progress, the area has already become alive with new visitors and users: runners, bicyclists, horse-back riders, gliders, families and kids, or brides and grooms taking their wedding day photos in the sunset.

Tindaya Project

Location:
Fuerteventura Island,
Canary Islands, Spain
Plan: 1994
Implementation:
Partially accomplished
Ordering party:
Canary Government
Project team:
Eduardo Chillida, José
A. Fernández-Ordóñez,
Daniel Díaz Font, Lorenzo
Fernández-Ordóñez
Collaborators:
Arup, Arup Geotechnics,
Scott Wilson; *consulting*:
Iberinsa Estudio Guadia
s.l.p.
Previous use: Mountain
Current use:
Being defined as a Sacred
Place/Sculpture
Surface:
250,000 cubic meters
Cost: 75 million euros

In 1994 the sculptor Eduardo Chillida had the opportunity to initiate the Tindaya Project in Fuerteventura, Canary Islands. A "work without materials" which opens a large interior space (approximately a cube with side length of 50 meters) in the heart of the mountain, so that it can "offer men of every race and color a great sculpture for tolerance." In 1984 Chillida had the idea of modifying the space of a quarry and transform it into a work of art. This vision materialized in Tindaya, when he realized that the work being done by the quarrymen, extracting stone from the mountain, was complementary with his own idea: that of introducing space into matter. The deriving synergy could be huge, as there were various quarries of ornamental stone that were slowly scratching and therefore damaging the mountain's surface. This idea of introducing space into matter is present in almost all of Chillida's artistic works, not only in his drawings and engravings, but also in his works of stone and steel, whose start dates back to his first pieces of alabaster. To create a space means to set limits, to delimit it, to define it: inserting a space or emptying it. For Chillida, to empty the heart of Tindaya means to create a space, between the sky and the earth, from where one can contemplate the horizon and abandon themselves to the light and the architecture created by the light itself. At that time—1994—Chillida needed, apart from the technical confidence provided by my father, the engineer José A. Fernández-Ordóñez, an architect capable of developing, fitting and visually presenting this idea he had been thinking over for such a long time. That was the start of my relationship with a project that not only is a powerful and unsurpassable sculpture, but also gives us a guideline to intervene on nature, thanks to the synergies this work implies. If there is a word that could define this project, that word is "integration." Integration between art and nature; integration between art and technique; space and economic development. Thanks to the Tindaya Project (and to the artist's observations and works), all the land surrounding the mountain, previously considered as a waste land of no value at all, is now valued as something precious. This is a desert area with no sustainable use, apart from its possible short length benefits as a land for building development, thanks to the huge demand for tourism of "sun and beach," whose expansion threatens the whole country.
Tindaya's Project makes us see the desert surrounding the mountain for what it is, an empty and essential place, as the sculpture itself, and presents the island with a monument of great personality and international scope, with a discourse that resembles the land itself: the sky and the earth, the silence and the horizon. It widens the cultural horizons of the land and can also be an engine of economic development.
By promoting the project, the Canary Islands authorities try to break the vicious circle of tourism and "sun and beach" urbanizations, and turn towards Art and Nature, putting everything on a quality touristic model (80% of the island's economy), in which the sculpture is the outstanding piece representing global interventions, as a sign of clarity, where a desert land is considered a communal good, instead of an object to be transformed. This area will now be a 100-square kilometer protected area, and the origin for the future National Park of *steppe* land in Fuerteventura. This project has revealed the true identity of a desert island to the inhabitants themselves, making them look, value, love their land for what it is, and as an investment for the future.

Skogskyrkogården

Location:
Stockholm, Sweden
Plan: 1915 (competition)
Implementation: 1917–40
Ordering party:
Cemeteries Authority
Project Team:
Gunnar Asplund
and Sigurd Lewerentz
Previous use: Quarry
Current use: Cemetery
Surface:
1.1 km² (267 acres)

Skogskyrkogården is a masterpiece among "recycled landscapes."
When Skogskyrkogården's architects Sigurd Lewerentz and Gunnar Asplund
designed the landscaping and the buildings, they started with the experience
of the land—previously a quarry—managing to create a "designed experience"
over the former nature of the site.
This is expressed in various ways. For example, the processional routes leading
to the chapels are designed to create the appropriate mood for mourners prior
to the funeral service. After the service, attention is drawn to the natural
surroundings, to help reconcile the mourners with the sadness of their loss
as part of the circle of life.
The clearest example is the Seven Springs Way leading up to the Chapel
of Resurrection, which is lined first with birches and then with conifers, the nearer
the mourners get to the chapel. The idea is that this will make them more somber
as they approach the chapel and the funeral ceremony. After the ceremony,
the mourners are led out of the chapel's west door and take a different path back.
This is meant to help them let go of their grief and gradually return to their normal
lives again.
Another example of the designed experience is represented by the steps
up to the meditation grove. Following the sloping terrain of the old quarry, each
step becomes lower and lower. This ensures that visitors are not tired out
by the climb, but instead feel calm when they reach this place of meditation.
Even minor details have been carefully considered. Although Sigurd Lewerentz
and Gunnar Asplund designed Skogskyrkogården together, the landscaping
was primarily the work of Lewerentz.
The landscaping is utterly unlike other cemeteries of the age, and is instead
clearly influenced by the pre-existing landscape conformation, with gentle hills,
space and openness.
Lewerentz also worked to imbue the landscape with plenty of contrasts: hills
and dips, dark and light and contrasting plants, still in line with the form of the old
quarry. This allowed him to design the cemetery according to the criteria specified
in the architects' competition Lewerentz and Asplund won in 1915.

Cava do Viriato

Location: Viseu, Portugal
Plan: 2000
Implementation: 2007–08
Ordering party:
Viseu Polis, SA
Project team: João Nunes,
Carlos Ribas
Collaborators: Iñaki Zoilo,
Joana Barreto, Cristina
Vasconcelos, Andrea
Alonso; *architecture:*
Gonzalo Byrne;
engineering: BETAR,
Estudos e Projectos de
Estabilidade, Lda Grade
Ribeiro, Estudos, Projectos
e Consultoria, Lda JOULE,
Projectos, Estudos
e Coordenação, Lda
Sojefer, Projectos
e Construções, Lda
Previous use: Quarry
Current use: Regeneration
of the Cava do Viriato
national monument;
environmental recovery
of the area
Surface: 1 km²
(253.8 acres)
Cost: 6.4 million euros

The project affects a very diverse territory and identifies some localized critical areas with very different structural conditions.
The space created for the Cava do Viriato through the enhancement of the public area of the monument is designed to ensure the functional integration of the site. The range of operations undertaken serve the common purpose of regenerating the public space in this area of the city, while acknowledging and seeking to promote the outstanding archaeological framework and landscape of the Cava do Viriato.
The chief aim of the project is to ensure the integrity and formal clarity of the monument, while laying down the rules for its direct fruition. Practically speaking, it rests on three fundamental aspects:
- the work carried out on the volume of the embankment (and trench, as its counterpart) is aimed to provide a micro-topographical recomposition, in an attempt to reverse the erosive processes that have been identified;
- the definition of a strategy for covering with plants the various surfaces of the volume, based on the monitoring of the micro-climate of each specific area, in particular according to two crucial vectors: the radiation received/exposure and the inclination of each sloping section. The result of this strategy is the choice of different coverings to mark the edges and make the geographical location of the site more easily recognizable—a crucial step to highlight the intrinsic significance of the monument;
- the definition of a functional connection with the exterior context and the introduction of a logic hinging on a visitor route combined with a rich cultural and recreational offering. This aim has essentially been expressed through the following aspects: a new definition of the circulation system; the clear marking of public spaces in the monument; the characterization of the exterior surroundings, with the basic assumption of suitably integrating the monument with the urban area; the creation of a coherent system of pedestrian paths,

with the aim of promoting a controlled fruition of the site on visitors' part
by connecting all the main parts of the monument.

The suggested solutions are inspired by the use of building materials and
techniques typical of the area, in relation to the choice of plants, the retaining
of the soil, and the types of paving adopted.

Finally, a limited range of materials—granite and Cor-ten steel—have been selected
and combined in such a way as to lend them greater complexity. The granite is used
in different ways, either alone or in combination with Cor-ten steel profiles.

It becomes a distinguishing feature of the paving, various sized blocks, cladding
of the edges of tree-planted areas, and gravel, as well as of stairways and walls.
The Cor-ten steel is instead used as a border-marker, set in close relation with
the built volumes, the service structures and the urban décor in the piazza.

The pathways are clad with a typical granite *calçada*, while the kerbs consist
of Cor-ten steel edges covered with granite gravel.

The existing tree and shrub covering has been the object of rigorous—almost
surgical—cleaning, maintenance and regeneration work. The embankments have
been consolidated and filled in order to erase the scars left by traces from
the Romantic period.

The embankments have been fully covered with non-irrigated grass, according
to their orientation and exposure to the sunlight and wind. The contrast with
the flat areas, consisting of an irrigated lawn, emphasizes the sloping planes.
Shrubs mark out the area of the piazza, while also protecting it from the adjacent
roads. The open spaces are characterized by lawns with a considerable
load-bearing capacity, as grounds for recreational and sporting activities.

The alignment of the trees brings out the outline of the diagonal pathways.
Provisions have been made to line the main roads with large trees with dense
leafage, to reduce the visual impact of traffic to a minimum.

100 ha

Rethinking the Landscape as the Meeting of Subjective Perception and Socio-Cultural Construction

Marina Ciampi and Paolo Chiozzi[1]

"Is the city still an anthropological place? This is no doubt a disturbing question if we interpret Marc Augé's notion of anthropological place literally, to mean a space that proves identity-building, relational and historical. These are all qualities that can hardly be attributed to the contemporary city, given the widespread standardization which 'citizens' inevitably perceive as excessive and, ultimately, as a threat to their identity, history, and usual ways of relating to others. The change in modes of social relation is perhaps the most worthy of attention on the viewer's part, if it is true—as has often been suggested—that the landscape contributes to defining them, while being at the same shaped by them." (Chiozzi 2001)

Any reflection on the subject of the landscape that aspires to avoid oversimplification from a scientific perspective must rely on forms of knowledge and practices related to those disciplines which have favored its development on the analytical level: architecture, urban planning, philosophy, anthropology, sociology, history, and geography. The intertwining of these forms of expertise contributes to widening the very notion of landscape, which is rather ambivalent in itself, since it brings into play a *subjective* dimension, understood as the individual perception of a given place, and an *objective* dimension, consisting of the things, elements and phenomena present within this geographical space. The polysemy of landscape is intrinsic to its constituting both an object of reference and its representation: as the former, it is a territorial system, the quality of a space possessing given morphological and environmental qualities; as the latter, it is the expression and representation of a contemplative mood, a source of feelings that may be conveyed by means of figurative or verbal languages.

The landscape is not something purely material; rather, it stems from the world of sensations: it is a territory which for complex (cultural, axiological, symbolical and mythological) reasons, through the presence of mankind, started being *rethought* (Raffestin 2005). The landscape, therefore, is the product of a *gaze* that is not primarily collective or social but rather individual, and which changes over time according to the codes used: the territory becomes a landscape the very moment in which one stops to gaze at (or photograph) it, thereby framing it within given cultural paradigms, forms of knowledge, and representations (Ciampi, in De Poli, Incerti 2013, p. 65). The landscape is thus a *complex* and *unitary* product whose origin lies—as Georg Simmel has shown—in *Stimmung*, i.e. that intellectual and spiritual disposition capable of providing an organic synthesis of all components: "Our conscience must acquire a new totality, something unitary which supersedes all elements, is not attached to their particular meanings and is not composed by them in a mechanical way—that is what landscape is." (Simmel 1913; It. transl. 2006, p. 53) While we cannot envisage nature as divided into parts, since it constitutes the unity of a totality witho no clear outlines (and so ceases to be nature in the absolute sense the moment something is removed from it), the opposite is true of the landscape: *delimitation*—being observed and understood within a temporary or long-lasting horizon—is absolutely crucial for it. When we are enveloped within the unity of nature, Simmel explains, there is no real separation between the perceiving ego and the seeing ego, since we always stand face to face with a landscape as *whole men*, capable of interpreting it according to the language produced by the community we belong to. These considerations bear some affinity to Edgar Morin's definition of *complexity*, understood as the combination of intertwining parts which only acquire meaning by virtue of their mutual *relations*: the observation of a complex system entails the role of an observer, who must reduce and simplify this complexity, without accessing the world "as it is."

It may be argued that man truly *inhabits* a territory only if he has produced a representation of it as a landscape. Besides, each individual combines body and consciousness, an organic structure and a cognitive one, and "is situated within a physical space that fully envelops him, but from which he can detach himself through his capacity to conceptualize it and recognize it as such." (Ciampi 2011, p. 10) The landscape, then, coincides with the full representation of our concrete living space, of the territory we have built and shaped as our dwelling place: it is always a form of nature, perceived or represented through a range of ideas, symbols, values and rules whose origins may be traced back to the historical subject. For this reason, we increasingly speak of a "culture of the landscape,"[2] to describe the reciprocal relation between man and his habitat, and the efforts made to develop projects as integrated and accessible as possible: we build for the future, to establish existence within the chronological framework of individual and social life, so as to enable future generations to make use of—and lend value to—what we have built. The *quality* of the landscape may be deeply affected by new forms of construction, reuse, recycling and superimposition that ultimately betray the identity of "insiders" and rob future generations of their inheritance—and thus *history*.[3] Eugenio Turri warns us of this aspect: "In order to draw man's attention, the landscape should roar at each wound inflicted upon it, like the provoked or injured beasts that primitive peoples have portrayed in their rock carvings [...] This tendency of man not to pay attention to the landscape, as though it were a fixed and indifferent stage, lies behind many of the disasters he causes through his way of living and acting detached from this very background [...] Man—especially Western man—is incapable of listening to the voice of the ecosystems he is part of; both an actor and factor within them, he is incapable of grasping the rhythms of those processes that extend back hundreds or thousands of years and bring landscapes to life." (Turri 2004, p. 23) With his anthropological reflections on the landscape, Turri opens up a new perspective in the search for a possible solution to the progressive and ongoing erosion of relations between man and the landscape: the latter is no longer perceived as a *fixed and indifferent stage*, but rather as a theater in which each person is required to play his or her part, as a *spectator* as well as actor.[4] Turri's aim is to draw attention to the socio-cultural consequences of living within an increasingly artificial landscape, of engaging in human activities that no longer entail a relation between man and nature: relations that no longer take place within a space clearly marked by natural elements and in which "the relations that matter are no longer, as in the past, those between man and nature, but rather those between men or societies." (Turri 2010, p. 122)

If one instead operates from the perspective of environmental sustainability and smart recycling, technology can show all its greatness and potential as a physical and cultural trace of the social system. Proof of this comes from High Line Park, which was developed through the regeneration of an old railway line first built in Manhattan in 1934 and dismantled in 1980: today it is a charming walkway that offers the visitor's gaze a view of key areas of the city.

A form of "recycling" such as this reflects strategies and policies aimed at recovering the social value and function of urban areas: as Alberto Schiavone notes, "the problem of politics has always been to integrate power—that of classes, nations, weapons, relations of production, and technology. Nowadays, vast techno-economical structures are already starting to redraw—in isolated and hence dangerous contexts—the civil and natural shape of the world. Soon they will be doing so in an even more substantial way. Politics cannot govern these structures, but must contribute to defining their direction, if it is still capable of envisioning projects. The only possible realism for it is anticipation." (Schiavone 2007, p. 89)

One political choice might be "non-intervention," but ultimately this is still a mode of intervention: the preservationist option is an artificial action compared to the spontaneous development of nature. For any landscape—as for all other fields of human action—it is best to adopt the ethics of responsible transformation, by laying down clear objectives and safeguarding fundamental social values: the protection of the territory as a nature park for all species, the safeguarding of its identity-building function, the shared enjoyment of the changes introduced. And the exact opposite is what occurred at Arbatax.[5]

The case of Arbatax
The 1960s witnessed the building of a real "cathedral in desert": a large paper mill created by politicians to promote the economic development of a depressed area. This development did occur, yet at what price? A spoiling of the landscape, for sure. But also the breakdown of a traditional community, which nonetheless reacted by giving itself a new identity: farmers, shepherds and fishermen became factory or office workers in a big company—they "built" a new identity for themselves. As one of them told me, "the paper mill brought Ogliastra out of the Middle Ages!". Not just Arbatax, not just the Municipality of Tortolì, but the whole area of Ogliastra. The factory soon triggered a radical transformation—a real social *mutation*, as Georges Balandier would describe it—that even managed to put

an end to the age-old isolation of the various communities of the Ogliastra area.[6] A process of social and cultural integration occurred, leading to an unprecedented degree of economic prosperity. The most significant aspect, from an anthropological perspective, however, was the emergence among local residents of a new way of perceiving themselves: no longer as shepherds or farmers resigned to a life of mere subsistence, but proud *paper manufacturers*. The same pride is to be found among paper workers in other areas of Italy, especially where the factories do not produce just any "paper" but particular kinds of paper.[7] The Arbatax paper mill chiefly manufactured paper for newspapers—and not just Italian ones either. Much of the paper, for instance, was exported to the Soviet Union, which in turn provided much of the timber required by the plant. This too is significant from a socio-anthropological perspective, since the crews of Soviet ships spent a considerable time in Arbatax and established friendly relations with local residents—particularly the paper workers. To this day, an important "landscape" trace is to be found in the paintings left by the Soviet seamen on the quayside.

The paper mill was closed after just thirty years. It was in the period of its final decline—also as a defining feature of the landscape—that I carried out my research.[8] Now in place of it a real desert extends: everything has been scrapped, and nothing has been built. It is as though someone had strewn the earth with salt—as the Romans did with Carthage after its destruction, to make the soil sterile.[9]

[1] The first part of this text was written by Marina Ciampi, while the Arbatax case is discussed by Paolo Chiozzi.

[2] The legislative frameworks too would appear to envision a broad, interdisciplinary scenario, since they transcend the purely formal and aestheticizing idea of landscape by bringing factors with more far-reaching implications into play, such as entrenched collective values, people's identity, and the natural environment: "The recent legislation suggests an extended approach to the landscape as the meeting ground between history and places, as the product of cultures that live in time and operate in space. These juridical documents may be described as the outcome of a long process of redefinition of a *cultural theme*, now resulting in a *cultural policy*." (Tosco 2007, pp. 8-9) In 2001 the European Community laid down the "European Landscape Convention"; in 2004 Italy drafted the "Code of Cultural Heritage and Landscape." The most interesting aspect that emerges from the latter document is the definition of the *cultural heritage* of the country, which includes not just monuments and artistic assets, but the sum of its cultural and landscape assets (art. 2 c. 1). Nature and history thus constitute collective assets to be safeguarded: the protection and promotion of the landscape is a way of safeguarding the values it conveys as tangible expressions of an identity.

[3] As early as 1973 Pierpaolo Pasolini had already expressed indignation at the outrages suffered by the city of Orte, whose natural and urban skyline had been disfigured through the addition of incongruous elements (see the short video *Pasolini e... la forma della città*).

[4] Turri uses the metaphor of the theater "in the Greek sense of *théatron*, which derives from *thàsasthai* = to contemplate, gaze at as a spectator, and hence suggests the position man finds himself

in when, leaving the fray of living behind [...] he stops to look." (Turri 2010, p. 27)

[5] Arbatax is a seaside town in the Municipality of Tortolì, in the Province of Ogliastra, on the east coast of Sardinia. The building of the paper mill also contributed to its development as a tourist resort, another significant factor of socio-economic and cultural transformation.

[6] Aside from coastal towns such as Arbatax, the province includes rural and mountain areas, which traditionally relied on a pastoral economy.

[7] During the fieldwork, two short films were produced: *La cartiera ad acqua "Il Paradisino"* and *La carta a mano (Cartiera Magnani)*: research by Paolo Chiozzi, filming and editing by Luca Managlia, sound recording by Guido Bresaola.

[8] This research was conducted together with photographer Davide Virdis and documentary-maker Sandro Nardoni in the years 2009–10.

[9] The visual-anthropological research on the Arbatax paper mill and its workers has yet to be published, with the exception of a short article by P. Chiozzi (*L'anima della cartiera: Memoria e identità per un territorio e i suoi abitanti*), a text written to accompany the exhibition by the same title that was held in Tortolì in April-May 2010, with photographs by Davide Virdis. However, a film-documentary has been made, *Papermakers Generation* (director: Sandro Nardoni; ethnographic research: P. Chiozzi; photography: D. Virdis; production and distribution: Concept, Florence).

Bibliography

B. Balandier, *Sociologie des mutations*, Anthropos, Paris 1970.

M. Ciampi, *Forme dell'abitare. Un'analisi sociologica dello spazio borghese*, Rubbettino, Soveria Mannelli 2011.

M. Ciampi, "Il territorio come bene sociale. Il paesaggio come spazio umanizzato," in M. De Poli, G. Incerti (eds.), *Trasformazioni. Storie di paesaggi contemporanei*, LetteraVentidue, Syracuse 2013.

P. Chiozzi, "Il territorio: luogo antropologico di indagine fotografica," in O. Goti, S. Lusini (eds.), *Strategie per la fotografia. Incontro degli archivi fotografici* (Proceedings of the conference held at Archivio Fotografico Toscano, Prato, 30 November 2000), Archivio Fotografico Toscano, Prato 2001.

P. Chiozzi, "Per un profilo antropologico dei cartai," in C. Cresti (ed.), *Itinerario museale della carta in Val di Pescia*, Edizioni Periccioli, Siena 1986.

E. Morin, *La méthode. Tome 3. La Connaissance de la connaissance*, Éditions du Seuil, Paris 1986.

C. Raffestin, *Elementi per una teoria del paesaggio*, Alinea editrice, Florence 2005.

A. Schiavone, *Storia e destino*, Einaudi, Turin 2007.

G. Simmel, "Philosophie der Landshaft" (1913), in *Gesamtausgabe*, Suhrkamp, Frankfurt, vol. 12.

C. Tosco, *Il paesaggio come storia*, il Mulino, Bologna 2007.

E. Turri, *Il paesaggio e il silenzio*, Marsilio, Venice 2004.

E. Turri, *Il paesaggio come teatro. Dal territorio vissuto al territorio rappresentato*, Marsilio, Venice 2010.

Umi-no-Mori

Location:
Tokyo Bay (Eastern section
of the Inner Central
Breakwater Reclamation
Area), Japan
Plan: 2007
Implementation:
2007 (kick off event,
planting start)
Ordering party:
Foundation of Midori no
Tokyo (Green Tokyo
fundraising campaign)
Project team:
Tadao Ando Architect
& Associates
Collaborators:
500,000 people
Previous use: Landfill site
Current use: Sea forest
Surface: 88 ha (217 acres)
Cost:
500 million Japanese yen
(only includes the value
of the trees, the planting
is done by volunteers)

In preparation for becoming the host of the 2016 Tokyo Olympics and with
a vision of transforming Tokyo into an ecological (environment friendly) city
in the span of ten years, an urban restructuring initiative has been considered.
Unlike the conventional urban development method of creating roads
and buildings, the aim was to generate a symbiosis between the artificial
and natural environment.
One of the initiatives, called "Green Corridors/Wind Passages" has been
underway since 2007. The idea was to create a green network in Tokyo
by connecting several existing large-scale green areas in the city and incrementing
the amount of tree-lined streets and boulevards.
Umi-no-Mori (Sea Forest), one of the cornerstones of this green network,
is expected to become a symbol of Tokyo's restructuring project. In a 100-hectare
landfill made out of industrial waste, located in the central breakwater off Odaiba
in the Tokyo Bay, we are people have been asked to donate 1000 yen each
for planting trees, with the aim of transforming this garbage mountain
into a forest on the sea. The birth of the Sea Forest will become a strong
message for the upcoming Century of the Environment.

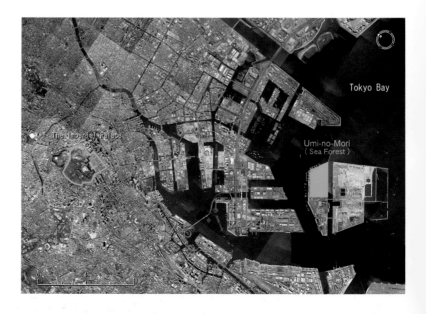

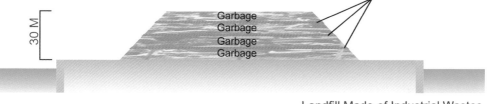

Landfill from Construction Sites

30 M

Garbage
Garbage
Garbage
Garbage

Landfill Made of Industrial Wastes

Tree Planting through Fund-raising

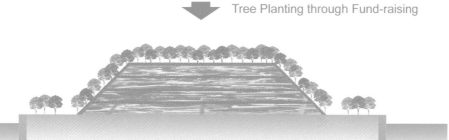

Umi-no-Mori
(Sea Forest)

Umi-no-Mori (Sea Forest) Cross Section Diagram

Landscape Restoration of the Vall d'en Joan Landfill Site

Location:
Garraf, Barcelona, Spain
Plan: 2002
Implementation: 2003–10
Ordering party:
AMB, Entitat Metropolitana
de Serveis Hidràulics
i Tractament de Residus,
Barcelona District
Project Team:
Enric Batlle, Joan Roig
(architects); Teresa Galí,
(agricultural engineer)
Collaborators:
Proser, Proyectos y
Servicios, S.A., Geocisa,
R.D.S., Jordi Nebot, Xavier
Ramoneda, Mario Suñer
(architects); Elena Mostazo,
(agricultural engineer)
Contractor:
Urbaser, Fcc, Cespa,
Comsa, Emte
Previous use: Landfill site
Current use: Public park
Surface:
85 ha (210 acres) surface;
20 ha (49 acres) built
surface
Cost: 11 million euros

The Vall d'en Joan is situated in the Natural Park of Garraf, in the municipalities of Beguesand Gavà, in the county of Baix Llobregat. Originally, this spot was one of the many closed, winding valleys that form the foothills of the Garraf massif. Its use as a landfill dates back to 1974, since when it has been the destination of most of the urban waste produced by Barcelona and its metropolitan area. When closure of the site began, this occupied an approximate extension of 85 hectares and had been filled to two-thirds of its original level.
The landfill restoration project aimed to address with a single operation the three basic aspects identified: solving a complex technical problem, creating a new public space and constructing a new landscape. The multidisciplinary technical team that carried out restoration brought to this single intervention knowledge from different disciplines (environmental engineering, geology, landscape architecture and agronomy) in order to create this new place.
The complex technical problems that derived from closing and capping the landfill served to outline a working strategy based on rationalization. The lay-out of stabilizing terraces and retaining embankments and the track providing access marked out the geometry of the landfill, and structured the layout of the piping meant to collect and conduct biogas to the transformation plant where the biogas is turned into electrical energy and the draining and storage of leachates. This organization was complemented by the construction of channels to divert runoff.
Of the three original objectives, the third, the construction of a new landscape, was influenced by a particular desire to integrate the former landfill into Garraf Natural Park. Obviously, the then morphology of the site was completely different to its original state. However, in other areas of Garraf there are cultivated valleys that have been modified by means of agricultural techniques adapted to the geography of the place, with systems of terrace construction, drainage and farming that were very similar to the technical steps necessary for the closing and capping of the landfill. This conversion of a landfill into a farming landscape was based on three key factors: topography, hydraulics and vegetation. The topographic system was addressed by the capping project. While the project for closure of the landfill involved channels and embankments, the landscape restoration project had recurred to farmed terraces, tree-planted plots and fields of crops. The hydraulic requirements for the implantation of the new landscape had to be addressed in the project. The various drainage systems existing on the series of terraces were used for this purpose, channeling rainwater to cisterns that we inserted in the banks of the landfill, and the irrigation system was run on the energy produced by the transformation of biogas.
Finally, for the replanting of the site we used resistant native species that require little water and can easily adapt to the environment. The vegetation introduced includes a range of bramble, scrub and Mediterranean maquis, trees and shrubs, and native leguminous crops in reference to the surrounding mosaic of farmland and woods, promoting the succession of the primary ecosystems on the site, which will, in time, develop and adapt to the environment.

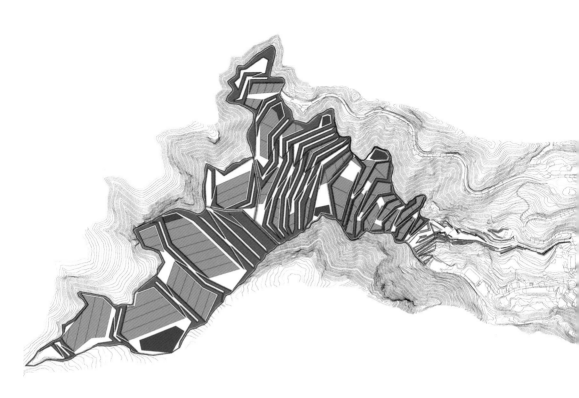

Zollverein Park

Location: Essen, Germany
Plan:
Master Plan 2002;
landscape design 2005
Implementation:
2003–06 Forum, Parking
A1; 2006–12 all other
outdoor installations
Ordering party:
Stiftung Zollverein, Essen;
Nrw.Urban GmbH & Co.
KG, Dortmund
Project team:
Master Plan: Agence Ter;
landscape design:
Planergruppe Oberhausen
Collaborators:
Art: Observatorium;
orientation system:
F1rstdesign; *lighting
design:* Licht Kunst Licht
Previous use:
Steel industry
Current use: Public park
Surface:
approx. 80 ha (198 acres)
Cost:
approx. 10 million euros

The history of Zollverein Park dates back to the 1990s. Before the extraction of coal and the completion of coke production, the area around the winding towers and coke batteries was an unappreciated landscape, a forgotten space: a no man's land where flora and fauna were rather furtive; humans were to be found rarely, particularly since the former work place got fenced off, immured and secured against intruders: a restricted area in an urban environment. With the end of the coal and coke production, nature began to grow: birches and shrubs, ferns and moss covered the area with a green-colored carpet. As nucleus of the Zollverein Park, the area of the coal settling pond and of the coal mine was clearly identified: a multiform free space in the surroundings of an unusual industrial area with light birch groves, dark bushes, and reflecting water surfaces, as well as wide open areas on black substrate. A fascinating place on a soil relief consisting of embankments, dams, hollows, crests, ramps and levels, framed by the scenery of high chimneys, cooling towers, the brick ashlars of the works of Schupp and Kremmer, and power poles. Right into this scenery, Ulrich Rueckriem positioned a large sculpture made out of Austrian granite and originating from the coal production. A significant place emerged, and became an element of the Kassel Documenta 1992. The formerly restricted area opened up slowly and became more and more accessible, enriched with familiar elements, bridges and stairs, and paths made out of dark substrate led to more sculptures and open new landscapes. A park developed, with the growing of trees, bushes, ferns and moss, without ignoring the meaningfulness of Rueckriem's sculptures. A second developing phase for the open spaces of the former Zeche Zollverein

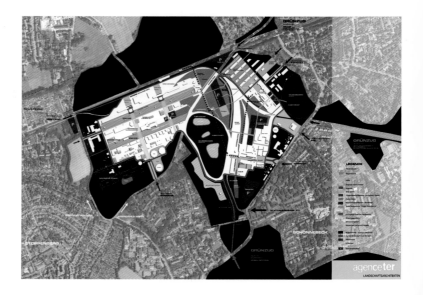

started with the repair and the change of the buildings of Pit XII during the IBA Emscher Park. Inside the old buildings and the power station, Sir Norman Foster and the architects Heinrich Böll and Hans Krabel built studios, the Design Centre with exhibition surfaces and meeting areas, and a restaurant. The exterior installations were carefully aligned and arranged: in particular, footpaths, places for visitors and car parking lots in the close surroundings of the buildings.

The beginning metamorphosis of the location was strengthened in a third phase with the development of a Master Plan by Rem Koolhaas: a goal was being defined for the urban development. With the new building of the Design School and the change of the coal wash, the first architectural indications were set.

A further Master Plan for the free space of Agence Ter/Henri Bava was the necessary addition to the urban planning by Rem Koolhaas: this Master Plan for the free space was specified in supplementing drafts.

The working team, consisting of landscape architects (Planergruppe GmbH, Oberhausen), artists (Observatorium, Rotterdam), communication designers (F1rstdesign, Cologne), and light designers (Licht Kunst Licht, Bonn), qualified during an international competition for this planning in the year 2005. As a result, the long-term experience and planning of Planergruppe Oberhausen could be carried out and developed accordingly.

A park developed, while at the same time stressing the existing industrial-architectural ensemble. The landscape architecture made use of the existing vegetation and terrain structure, in order to create a scenary able to emphasize industrial elements as naturally as possible.

Adlershof Nature Reserve and Recreation Park

Location:
Treptow, Berlin, Germany
Plan: 1996 (competition)
Implementation:
1997–2005
Ordering party:
Auftraggeber Berlin
Adlershof
Aufbaugesellschaft
Project Team:
Büro Kiefer
landschaftsarchitektur
Collaborators:
Erik Ott, Tancredi Capatti,
Katja Erke, Sybille Lacheta,
Andreas Westendorf
Previous use: Airport
Current use: Public park
Surface: 70 ha (173 acres)

The nature reserve and recreation park on a former airfield in Adlershof, Berlin, is situated right in the center of the Science and Commerce City. The concept suggests a clearly articulated park with active and landscape zones. Germany's first civilian engine-powered aircraft took off from the airfield in the early 20th century. But after two world wars and the division of the city, the airfield was abandoned. The attached science and media infrastructure, though, stayed in the area. The airfield itself became an extensively used square-bashing area and was covered over by pioneer vegetation. The site developed to a diverse biotope for urban flora and fauna.

The core of the park retains the character of a dry grassland biotope. Making history visible reinforces the identity of the place. "Design that ignores historical connections remains abstract and theoretical, and misses the opportunity to discover the poetry of the place," insists Gabriele Kiefer in a discussion with writer and journalist Thies Schröder. This area is now legally designated a nature conservation area, and is accessible only via raised wooden walkways. But the active area of the park, which forms a transition to the surrounding town, is created in the form of park chambers—bordered by lines of trees—which follow the ground plan of the Science and Commerce City and are meant for various uses. A "spatial framework" is created for future uses that are not yet fixed. "I offer the frame, and the users provide the filling, that is how good parks come into being." The frame also changes the way visitors look at the dry grassland: this is suddenly perceived as high value nature.

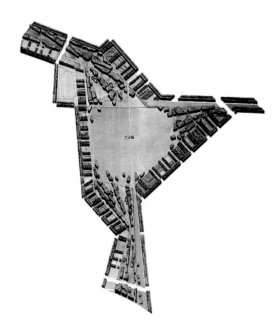

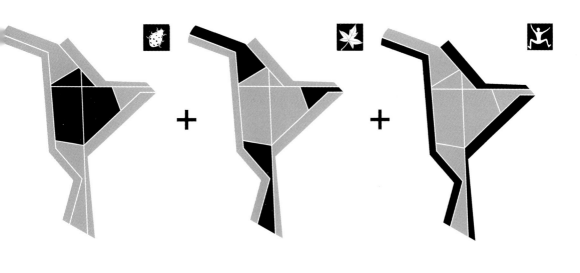

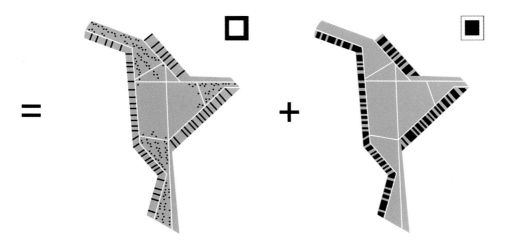

Hong Kong Wetland Park

Location:
Tin Shui Wai, New Territories, Hong Kong, China
Plan: 1998–2006
Implementation: 2006
Ordering party:
Agriculture, Fisheries and Conservation Department Hong Kong SAR Government, China
Project team:
Architectural Services Department Hong Kong SAR Government
Previous use:
Agricultural land
Current use: Wetland
Surface:
61 ha (152 acres); 1 ha Visitor Centre Building Area
Cost: 518 million HK dollars

The site of Hong Kong Wetland Park (HKWP) was originally intended as an ecological mitigation area (EMA), to compensate for the wetlands lost due to Tin Shui Wai New Town development. The EMA not only serves as a buffer between Tin Shui Wai and the internationally important wetlands of the Mai Po Inner Deep Bay Ramsar Site to the northeast, but also functions as a world-class conservation, education and tourism facility that shows the functions and values of wetlands for use by over 2.6 million local and overseas visitors since its opening in May 2006.

The 61-hectare HKWP provides a wide range of habitats, including constructed freshwater, brackish and inter-tidal wetlands, reed beds, grassland, mangrove, shrubland and woodlands.

Construction materials were re-used or recycled. Structural concrete containing recycled aggregates or pulverized fuel ash (PFA) as partial cement replacement was used—this amounted to approximately 75% of the total concrete volume; the majority of the recycled aggregates were generated from a nearby recycling plant. The ground paving near the entry plaza used recycled granite materials. Chinese bricks from demolished old houses were used to construct a brick wall on the south front of the Visitor Center and ticket office, with the aim of mitigating solar gain of the building. In addition, old timber fenders of piers were used as perching posts for birds in the freshwater marshes, and oyster shells sourced from the nearby Lau Fau Shan oyster farm were also used for the fences.

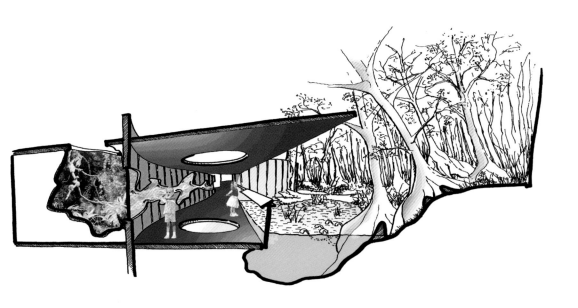

樹林
WOODL

現有之西河道
EXISTING WESTERN

演替之
SUCCESSION WA

濕地
WETLAND DISCOVE

溪畔漫遊
STREAM W

停車
CAR PA

接待中心
RECEPTION CENTRE

天水圍
TIN SHUI WAI

N

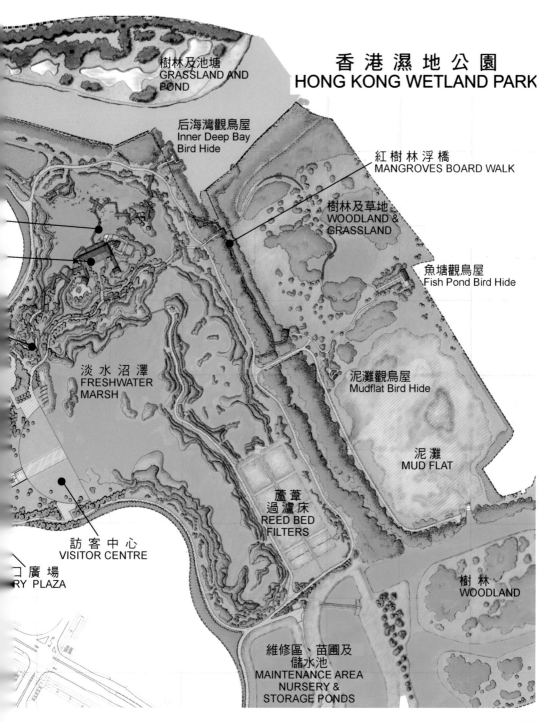

香港濕地公園
HONG KONG WETLAND PARK

樹林及池塘
GRASSLAND AND POND

后海灣觀鳥屋
Inner Deep Bay Bird Hide

紅樹林浮橋
MANGROVES BOARD WALK

樹林及草地
WOODLAND & GRASSLAND

魚塘觀鳥屋
Fish Pond Bird Hide

淡水沼澤
FRESHWATER MARSH

泥灘觀鳥屋
Mudflat Bird Hide

泥灘
MUD FLAT

蘆葦過濾床
REED BED FILTERS

樹林
WOODLAND

訪客中心
VISITOR CENTRE

口廣場
RY PLAZA

維修區、苗圃及儲水池
MAINTENANCE AREA NURSERY & STORAGE PONDS

50 ha

New Territories Sub Specie Artis
Adriana Polveroni

There are two opposite poles, one constituted by a brutal terrorist attack, the other by an even more brutal tale of terror. Yet even these two black holes have been transformed, in conformity with the requirement for a change of use, for the renovation of places and their functions which marks the accelerated time of our age. Ground Zero in New York, which opened up amid death and ruin on 11 September 2001, has been filled by a sinuous vertical creature. Was it not the case that behind it lay years of debate and stagnation, it might strike us not as the most recent and bold skyscraper of the Big Apple, but as an unreal picture whose height blots out the chasm created by the collapse of the Twin Towers. The other black hole has never been a physical gap; rather, it is an abyss in the memory of 20th-century Europe and—at the same time—one of its most paradoxical symbols: the former industrial plant in which Oskar Schindler crowded Polish Jews to save them from the gas chambers. Today this is the site of the contemporary art museum of Krakow, the MOCAK. It is not a particularly attractive building, but it is certainly chilling, as it implicitly raises a series of questions on art: why does this often come to life where a negation of life itself has occurred? Is this a sign of cynicism or of a capacity—greater than that of any other human language or attitude—toshape new identities?

To tell the truth, in both cases architecture replaces the memory of those black holes by turning them into venues for entertainment, trade and cultural offerings. This architecture, however, is highly indebted to art, if for no other reason than the fact that here is where "beauty" has moved to in recent decades—classical beauty, in a way, where "beautiful form" is what matters. The latter is no longer the exclusive domain of art, but rather of the planning of space, on a large or small scale: of design and architecture.

In order to briefly outline the geography of that process of transformation of places that is commonly carried out by art, but even more often jointly activated by art and architecture, I have chosen to set out from the two opposite poles just described, which are highly symbolically charged. These are like two metaphors enclosing a vast range of examples and solutions sprung from very different places of origin. Generally speaking, the transformational capacity of art becomes more evident where it is required to solve a difficult situation, a practice which artists have especially taken up since the 1960s. In this decade they sought to address the issue of public space, *also* because of the need to abandon the "protected"—and to some degree "suffocating"—space of the gallery or museum in order to create a kind of art consciously removed from the market. It was a matter of "straying" from what had been the venue for art over the past two centuries (the museum), so as to critically engage with the world.

Yet these are not the only cases in which art expresses its transformational inclination. Besides, nowadays this occurs less and less often as a free choice on artists' part (as in the 1960s), for the practice increasingly revolves around processes of negotiation with local areas in which other social actors come into play alongside artists and architects: institutions, local governing bodies, decision-makers, and—most recently—cultural planners, on top of the recipients of the projects. The outcome are complex arrangements aimed at the creation of new territories, be they urban or embedded in the natural landscape.

Personally, I have always been fascinated by the attempt to make an artwork of nature—an attempt in many ways as extreme as the two poles mentioned at the beginning. The nature at play here is not one wounded by the hand of man, or simply by the massive industrial processes that in the 20th century altered and often damaged the morphology and underlying spirit of an area. Rather, it is a pristine nature which still plays a central role—in the form of an isolated volcano (even a dormant one), for instance, or a river majestically running across a vast landscape. While art no longer has much to do with beauty, at times it strives to establish very close relations with the sublime, according to modes that are only apparently removed from the Romantic aesthetics of the sublime. What I have in mind here is the project which the American artist James Turrell has been working on for years with his *Roden Crater*: a "heroic" attempt to turn a volcano crater in Arizona into a workshop for pure light. Another example would be the attempt to partially cover the Arkansas River in Colorado which the Bulgarian-born artist Christo took up years ago with his wife Jeanne-Claude, who recently passed away.

Here the transformation, if ever completed, will have a merely "additive" character: it operates upon a natural context that is not altered in order to erase a pre-existing, negative memory, but which rather adds an identity *sub specie artis* to the natural identity of the place.

One successful example of this manipulative approach to art, intended to create an artificial reality almost as a match for the original beauty of nature, is *Montaña Tindaya*: a work which the Basque artist Eduardo Chillida has developed on one of the Canary Islands, Fuerteventura. "The idea was to create a sculpture that would protect the sacred mountain. The large space created in the heart of the mountain is invisible from the outside, but those who dare to venture within will see the sun and the moon from a hollow with no horizon," Chillida stated when illustrating his project in 1996. To accomplish it, 125,000 cubic meters of rock have been extracted from the mountain. This is partly an invasive operation, then, although it is meant to protect the sacredness of the site. It has not respected nature, at any rate according to the common meaning of this expression; rather, it has altered nature in the name of art.

A similar operation has taken place in Sicily with the open-air museum Fiumara d'Arte, a project first launched over twenty years ago by Antonio Presti. Here no mountains have been excavated, no rivers drained; the morphology of the area has not been remoulded, but tons of concrete have been poured to create the giant creatures now filling the Fiumara d'Arte.

These works have created a new skyline, one generally regarded as better than the natural one. The presence of these sculptures lends Fiumara its bewitching quality: they stand as the stern yet charming custodians of an area which is not so much degraded as simply neglected. Presti's project, however, lends symbolic value to the area extending from the foot of the Nebrodi mountains to the coastal stretch between Castel di Tusa (marked by Pietro Consagra's *La materia poteva non esserci*) and Villa Margi (dominated by Tano Festa's *Monumento a un poeta morto*)—as a denunciation of the overall state of neglect of Sicily, and especially of its coastline. In this respect, Fiumara d'Arte constitutes a rather unusual operation: it does not really reclaim a landscape or assign it a new and radically different identity, and only partially lends it a new function. However, it acts in a highly transformational manner, "bringing order" to the territory (a concept I will be further elucidating shortly), turning it into an artistic creation, the symbolic value of which exceeds that of the area enclosing it.

Yet a different case is that of Arte Pollino, the project that was launched in Basilicata in 2007. Here the choice was made to develop—alongside the local tourist industry—a cultural offering that would turn the Pollino National Park into an artistic destination. This is no landscape to be reclaimed by altering its morphological coordinates and use: the park is a natural asset which is strongly protected and rather suffers from a degree of isolation, because of its extensiveness and remoteness from large urban centers. Here too, then, the idea of "recycling" a landscape acquires an additive quality, since the creation of large environmental installations—such as those by Giuseppe Penone and Anish Kapoor (respectively *Teatro vegetale* and *Earth Cinema*)—or site-specific works (*RB Ride*, Karsten Höller's large carousel) is added on to the natural landscape, which remains unaltered.

By contrast, more explicitly transformational operations, jointly involving art and architecture, have mostly concerned the urban landscape in recent years. The range of examples is vast and ever-expanding, but I would like to focus on a couple of cases I am well-acquainted with. The new Waterfront in Seattle was developed in 2006 according to an architectural plan (drafted by the Weiss/Manfredi studio in New York) that breaks the frontal perspective by "terracing" it and making the area accessible through an open-air museum marked by Calder's iconic installation *The Eagle*. Aside from this, the site also features works by Richard Serra, Teresita Fernández, Mark Di Suvero, Mark Dion, Louise Bourgeois and Beverly Pepper, among other artists. The aim was to give the city a new area overlooking the sea, to replace the poor view of Seattle previously afforded by the waterfront.

The creation of a new waterfront is a common feature in recent urban regeneration schemes. In the case of this North American city, it fitted within the broader regeneration policy, which especially concerned the creation of new landmarks that would change the face of Seattle—from unattractive, remote city to an anthology of open-air architecture. Here with the Central Library Rem Koolhaas has (arguably) created his most accomplished project, while Steven Holl has designed a "textbook" church (St. Ignatius

Chapel) and Frank Gehry has developed a small Guggenheim: the Experience Music Project.

The Municipal Administration of Turin has also chosen to promote a new urban vision that would redesign a city shaped by its industrial past. The driving factors have been the 2006 Winter Olympics and, even more so, the crisis of the automobile sector, which for years had represented the main growth stimulus for the city. Among other projects intended to redefine the face of Turin according to the administrators' plans—as well as its economy as a center of cultural and hence non-material production— we find the interring of the railway line that cuts across the city from north to south. The new route, designed by Vittorio Gregotti, has also come to serve as the axis for the development of a new open-air museum (the completion of which has been delayed by the 2008 crisis) with works by artists the likes of Giuseppe Penone and Per Kirkeby, and Mario Merz's large *Igloo* as an ideal starting point.

It is indeed in cities, rather than in natural settings, that the transformational inclination of art has best expressed its potential. Leaving aside the visionary qualities of artists such as Turrell and Christo, who really push the limits of what is feasible and conceptually transcend the perspective of "landscape recycling" in their work, it is worth noting that over the years projects developed in uninhabited areas have proven precarious because of the lack of targeted end users. These projects retain a strongly relational character, albeit not always explicitly so; and in order for them to be fully accomplished, there must be some actors who can *activate* them, thereby marking their positive outcome. Should these conditions not be met, the outcome will only amount to a formal redefinition of the landscape, incapable of assigning it a new use and hence of lending it new life.

The most telling example, in this regard, is provided by the largest open-air museum in Europe, and possibly the world: the Nordland Artscape in Norway, which extends between the city of Bodø and the Lofoten Islands in the Arctic Circle. The remarkable efforts made by the local administration, with the support of the Norwegian government, to create a route of hundreds of kilometers punctuated by sculptures and installations has not been enough to revitalize an area doomed to isolation because of its vastness, remoteness, and harsh climate. Former fishermen's houses in the Lofoten were assigned to theater companies and turned into ateliers, in order to draw an international public of artists. The aim was to attract new residents and create a sort of *cordon sanitaire* around Nordland Artscape, consisting of people and the practices they engage in. Only once Stamsund, a town of just 1500 inhabitants, opened the Nordland Visual Theater, featuring national and international performances, did the Lofoten become a destination for short-term residents—on top of its (few) tourists.

To end these brief observations, I wish to present a question—not a solution—that is implicitly raised by the various cases discussed in this volume. Nowadays—and practically always, I would argue—art constitutes an attitude and language which ensures the possibility of leaving a strong imprint on reality. Art has the power to alter the conceptual perspective from which we gaze at the world, making change possible. In this respect, art is an "ordering" language, which achieves a synthesis even when the starting point is the "disorder" created, for instance, by massive processes of industrialization and spontaneous or illegal urbanization. However, art is also "pliable," insofar as it "adapts" to the realities it operates upon. It therefore possesses a "hetero-transformational" capacity; but at the same time, it seems to me to be marked by a "self-transforming" capacity, in the sense that it adapts and submits to a wide range of possible solutions. The "pliability" of art, then, is twofold: it operates as a principle for redefinition, which lends things a new order, a new identity. And in doing so it renews its original nature as a means of crafting, as the *poiesis* that distinguishes the artistic approach—and which finds concrete, as well as theoretical, expression as a new outlook on the world.

Zittau-Olbersdorf Landscape Park

Location:
Lake Olbersdorf - north
shore, city of Zittau /
municipality Olbersdorf,
Germany
Plan: 1995–99
Implementation: 1999
Ordering party:
LGS Zittau-Olbersdorf 1999
GmbH
Project team:
Rehwaldt
Landschaftsarchitekten:
Heike Langkutsch (project
leader), M. Kronberg,
J. Bräunlein, D. Rehdanz,
S. Fauck, C. Rindt,
K. Strobel, C. Tümpel
Previous use: Mine
Current use: Public park
Surface: 30 ha (74 acres)
Cost: 4.8 million euros

For over two hundred years the Zittau basin has been a vast surface brown coal mining area. Surface mining expanded and changed the historical cultural landscape completely, like never before. Villages and towns were erased, forests cut down, whole regions were drained. With the end of the mining in the 1990s new perspectives arose for the development of the Zittau region during the discussion about the future of this type of landscape.

In 1994 the city of Zittau and the community of Olbersdorf were designated as the premises for the Second Saxon state garden exhibition in 1999. The concept intended to develop the area on both sides of the Mandau, a former river meadow, into a green park connected to the open landscape. Another idea was to flood the mining hole and to develop a recreation area beside the lake, which could be connected with the settlements around.

North of the river there is a park full of old trees—called Zittau west park—which was used for the festival. On the south, in the former mining area the chance arose to develop a totally new landscape. This very contrast—here the old park as a well-known situation and there the dusty hole as the new that is forthcoming—became the program of the show.

The idea behind the exhibition and its setting in Zittau and Olbersdorf was to develop an extensive landscape-park, which documents the changes of the landscape after the end of the mining activities, and with the newly-introduced modern design. The former mine facilities on the north side of the flooded lake in front of the great scenery of the Zittau mountains are the focus of the showground.

In the Olbersdorf Landscape Park the history of the landscape is still present. Remains from the old cultural landscape, slopes, brooks, old trees—like rare fossils—are exhibited in the surrounding. The still present mining equipment gives the site its specific character. The autonomy of these "fragments of the landscape" is carefully respected. New design elements are added to the basic model and fit in conveniently. The intensively-designed lake shores are part of the recreation area on the bathing lake.

Despite the big variety of the site the role of the former coal mine is always present as a center point. The "mining" topic is the ideological clamp that keeps the site as a whole.

Nature returns: in a few years, the objects which today are standing *en plein air* will be overgrown by bushes and forests. The site will then get its own new value and become a document of a past time.

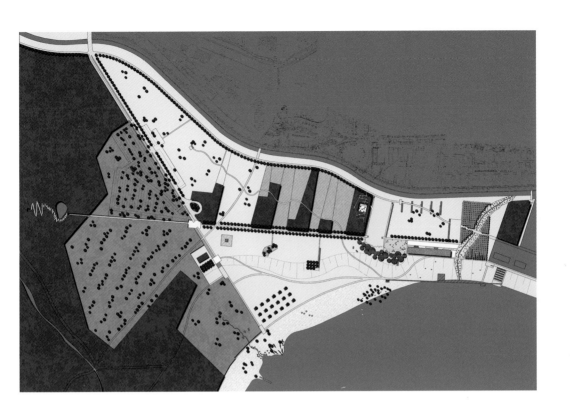

Former Saltern at La Rochelle

Location:
La Rochelle, France
Plan: 1967–70
Implementation: 1970
Ordering party:
City of La Rochelle, France
Project team:
André Gomis (member
of the ATUA - Atelier
d'Urbanisme
et d'Architecture, lead
architect for the City
of La Rochelle); Martine
Guiton (state-registered
architect and landscape
designer, landscape
architect in charge
of the work)
Previous use: Saltern
Current use: Nature park
Surface: 30 ha (74 acres)

The recovery aspect is represented by the creation of a 30-hectare stretch of water upstream from the city of La Rochelle, near the "new city" of Périgny-Aytré, in the area where the old abandoned saltern is located had various aims:
- restore a semi-industrial landscape and reclaim salt-contaminated land;
- create a park for residents of the new city nearby;
- channel the existing small river, the Moulinette;
- collect the run-off water produced by the recent building work (roads, car parks, roofs, etc.) through soil sealing, in such a way as to avoid flooding the city of La Rochelle downstream.

Only one map was available: the Land Registry map recording all the parcels. An analysis of this document made it possible to detect the presence of typical narrow plots, along with a series of channels and ponds with regular shapes. The surveys began. This was a vast abandoned area, extending across 30 hectares, 5 kilometers away from the sea. Its windswept fields, white with salt, hosted rows of spindly, curved trees: almost century-old tamarisks lined the channels, while growing all around the ponds of the old saltern was the common reed, a low-lying plant typical of damp areas and capable of growing on salty soil. One of the distinctive features of the site which was important to preserve was the existing vegetation. Few new plants would manage to survive there.

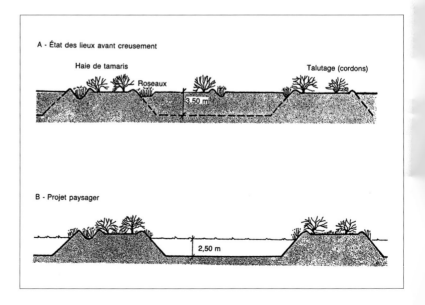

A - État des lieux avant creusement

Haie de tamaris   Roseaux   Talutage (cordons)

3,50 m

B - Projet paysager

2,50 m

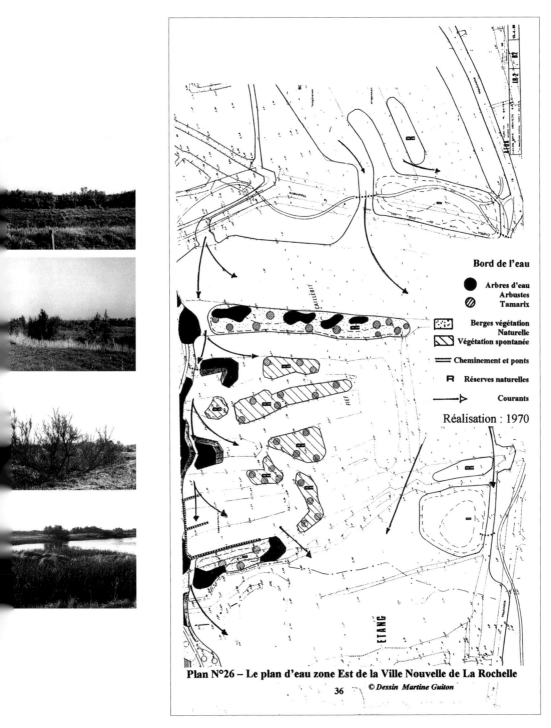

Bord de l'eau

⬤   Arbres d'eau
          Arbustes
◍   Tamarix

▓   Berges végétation
          Naturelle
▨   Végétation spontanée

═   Cheminement et ponts

Я   Réserves naturelles

→   Courants

Réalisation : 1970

Plan N°26 – Le plan d'eau zone Est de la Ville Nouvelle de La Rochelle

36   © *Dessin Martine Guiton*

Main aims were:
- to create *islands* to preserve the rows of tamarisks. The choice of preserving
these rows of trees led to the creation of *oblong* islands, in such a way
as to preserve as many trees as possible;
- to create some *currents* along the banks, in such a way as to avoid
the proliferation of mosquitoes and the stagnation of floating residues;
- to develop a stretch of water with a *curvy outline*, giving the impression
of being an ancient natural basin;
- to give it a depth of 2.50 meters, so as to avoid the proliferation of seaweed
(by excavating certain sections accordingly).

A single plan was drawn for the project. The stretch of water was traced directly
on a Land Registry map measuring 2 × 1 meters. This map showed the position
of the small channels (lined by rows of tamarisks) and the exact location
of the ponds from the old saltern (surrounded by groves of reeds).
A single representative cross-section was used for shaping the banks, which were
excavated with a 45° slope to a depth of 2.50 meters, while uniformly maintaining
a height of one meter above the ground in order to contain floods and avoid any
overflowing.
The work soon led to the creation of a natural setting marked by the presence
of a large stretch of water with an extension of 30 hectares.
The existing marsh vegetation was preserved on the surface of the newly-created
islands.

The islands already filled with tamarisks and the bank ridges covered with compressed compost were intended to ensure a twofold saving:
- saving on new plants, given the presence of a sturdy vegetation requiring no gardening or watering;
- saving in terms of the need to create new embankments, thanks to the preservation of the old canals.
Forty years on, the islands still require no gardening or replenishing of the vegetation.

Unexpected changes
Both sedentary and migratory birds have chosen these islands as havens and nesting areas despite the surrounding urban sprawl (apartment blocks and detached houses). The birds knew they would be safe from vandalism here.
What hadn't been foreseen but was discovered in 1990—twenty years after the completion of the project—were the choreographies created on the surface of the water by the flight and landing of dense flocks of birds: a highly popular attraction among the inhabitants of the city, and one which has since been taken up by some large amusement parks as well.
The success of this vast project of artificial development, which has recreated a totally natural ecosystem within such a difficult environment, has proved really amazing.
And all this, with just one map, just one cross-section...

Buttes-Chaumont

Location: Paris, France
Plan: 1863–65
Implementation: 1863–67
Ordering party: Conseil municipal
Project team: Jean-Charles Adolphe Alphand and Pierre Barillet-Deschamps, under Georges-Eugène Hausmann's supervision
Previous use: Gypsum quarry
Current use: Public park, botanical garden
Surface: 25 ha (61.8 acres)

Located in the farthest outskirts of Paris, the Buttes-Chaumont Park has a complex history: an execution site in the distant past, it became first a public abattoir, then a quarry, and finally a public rubbish dump. This 25-hectare site was a sterile and disjointed area, cut off from the city. Moreover, the quarrying had made one large hole of it, with sudden drops, vast crevices and jagged faults.
The engineering work carried out by Jean-Charles-Adolphe Alphand and Gabriel Davioud turned these drawbacks into strategic points for the landscape. Through what may be regarded as cutting-edge hydraulic operations for those years, the crevices and sharp rocks were reconfigured as part of the landscape.
This considerable transformation chiefly consisted of substantial morphological alterations, whose impact was further increased by the development of articulated pathways.
The outcome was an innovative park, combining technology, broad perceptual structures and the blending of natural elements within the very heart of a big city.

Parque da Juventude

Location:
São Paulo, Brazil
Plan:
2002–05 (national
competition: 1999)
Implementation:
Parque Esportivo: 2003,
Parque Central: 2004–05,
Parque Institucional: 2006–08
Ordering party:
São Paulo State
Government/Department of
Youth, Sports and Leisure
Project team:
Landscape architecture:
Rosa Grena Kliass
Arquitetura Paisagística
Planejamento e Projetos
Ltda.: Rosa Grena Kliass
(author); José Luiz Brenna
(co-author)
Collaborators:
Alessandra Gizella da Silva,
Gláucia Dias Pinheiro,
Mauren Lopes de Oliveira.
*Architecture and project
coordination:*
Aflalo & Gasperini
Arquitetos; *urban sign and
furniture design:* Univers
Arquitetura e Design;
lighting design: Senzi
Consultoria Luminotécnica;
structural engineering:
Escritório Técnico César
Pereira Lopes and CPOS;
*hydraulic and electrical
engineering:* MHA
Engenharia and CPOS;
*earthwork and drainage
engineering:* Rubens
Misorelli Engenharia de
Projetos and CPOS
Previous use: Jailhouse
Current use:
Public park and sports
facilities
Surface: 24 ha (59 acres)
Cost:
Sports Park: 7 million
brasizilian reals
Central Park: 6.5 million
brasizilian reals

The largest urban area in the country and one of the largest metropolitan areas in the world, São Paulo is a huge challenge for urban planners and designers. One of the main issues is the restoration of important misused urban sectors. This 24-hectare park is inserted in a consolidated urban sector, using part of a partially abandoned penitentiary complex.

The plan and the features of the site have led to the definition of three sectors: the Sports Park, the Central Park and the Institutional Park.

The first sector, the 35,000-square-meter Sports Park, has been set in a derelict area, once used as a rubble deposit. Along the axis of the Main Promenade, the area has ten sports courts and a skate court. A trail leads to small sitting areas, under the shadow of trees, sparing visitors the crossing of the entire area to reach the rest of the park. This sector is opened to the public in the evenings, and therefore its lighting design received a special care.

A significant area with a marquee is used to shelter the facilities and the snack bar and connects this sector with the Central Park.

This second sector was conceived with a naturalistic design, favoring natural features, groves of trees and extended lawns.

The peculiarity of this sector is the exploitation of a whole area with the abandoned structures of an unfinished prison. These structures, overgrown by a spontaneous grove of *Tipuana tipu*, resulted in a magic site and have been re-qualified by means of a wooden walkway with decorative elements in cor-ten steel and wood. This runs along the old walls and gives birth to an aerial walkway that can be reached by means of three staircases.

Beyond this unfinished building structures some remaining pieces of the walls and upper walks were linked by an iron passageway, reached by staircases, resulting in a 300-meter-long promenade, 6.5 meters out of which above the ground level. Here you can walk amid the trees canopies and enjoy the views of the park.

Contrasting with this dense site, the rest of the area, a vacant land, has been structured by modeling the land in mounds and vast lawns, reinforcing the naturalistic character and offering rest spaces.

Over the creek, a large bridge leads to the third sector: the Institutional Park. This is a large plaza, composed by the space among the four main buildings of the prison. Two of the buildings have been demolished and the other two were re-qualified into Community Services.

Here is the connection between the Park and the Metropolis. The subway touches the park with the Carandiru Station leading to the large plaza that represents the distribution point for the users.

Spoor Noord Park

Location:
Antwerp, Belgium
Plan: 2003–07
Implementation:
May 2008 (western part)
and June 2009
(eastern part)
Ordering party:
Antwerp City
Project team:
Studio Associato Bernardo
Secchi Paola Viganò, Milan,
Italy; Pieter Kromwijk,
Maastricht,
The Netherlands
Collaborators:
Competition: E. Alfier,
K. Arioka, K. Boon,
F. d'Agnano, G. de Roia,
U. Dufour, L. Fabian,
A. Moro, P. Ochelen,
G. Zaccariotto; *executive
project and yard:*
A. Carlesso, T. Fait,
S. Geeraert; *economic
feasibility:* Rob Cuyvers and
Frans Steffens; *mobility:*
Iris Consulting: Pieter
Kromwijk with D. Beys,
B. Schmähling,
A. Wierzchowska,
C. Menzel, E. Biesmans
Previous use: Railroad
Curent use: Public park
Surface:
24 ha (59 acres):
17 ha park, 7 ha built;
1.6 km of length
Cost: 14 million euros
(58.4 €/sqm - maintenance
costs: 120,000 €/year)

The project proposed by Studio 03 - Bernardo Secchi Paola Viganò had ambitious goals: in the idea of a *renovatio urbis*, Spoor Noord Park was conceived as an action with important effects not only for the decommissioned rail yards themselves but also for the neighborhood and the city itself. The different roles the park will play are contained in the motto "villages and metropolis": a park for the entire city, important for the metropolitan region and beyond; a park for the neighborhood and everyday activity. The transformation of the ex-railway platform used for the former port into a public park and mixed-used development should adhere to the following guidelines: maintain the east-west ecological connection through the park; concentrate new development in the western part, crossed by a green strip that can reach the Scheldt. The strategy is to change the role of the area from the city's backyard to a valuable part of Antwerp, fully expressing the neighborhoods' strong potential. The connection of the different parts of the city with the neighborhoods through the park is essential.

For this reason, the park is not a closed figure but it interweaves edges and internal areas in a unique spatial concept that relates the neighborhood to the Scheldt and to the docks. The underlying idea is that a park is a social space—a free space—which provides the population with an opportunity to create experiences and to be active. The main feature of Spoor Noord Park is its dimension: a vast and simply-designed lawn crossed by paths that can relate the neighborhoods with one another and with the park itself. Gardens, sports fields, transparent forests host many different formal and informal social activities and define multiple atmospheres.

Campus and fabric: the urban language of the western and densest part of the park is made up of contrasting figures—the bases of buildings, facades the same heights as the existing buildings, towers. The area could be defined as a "campus"—architectural objects freely located within a park. Or it could be defined by the new street facades. The project proposes two settlement principles: the campus and the fabric.

They are not conceived as two contradictory ideas but as possible (and even provisional) states in time.

lawn

lawn+gardens+forest+patio gardens

lawn+gardens

lawn+gardens+forest+patio gardens+sportfields

lawn+gardens+forest

lawn+gardens+forest+patio gardens+sportfields+main path

A social space
The form, the role and the meaning of a park have changed in the past and are continuously changing. The park today is a new social space. Without neglecting the past it is, firstly, a site of many social everyday practices and, secondly, an important urban element contributing to give the whole city and metropolis a clear spatial structure.

Our main ideas follow a bottom-up path: starting from what we, as individuals or as collectivity, do in a park. Obviously the transformation of such an important part of the city leads to more general reflections on its role in Antwerp.

A new geography is modifying weights and relations among its different parts: the dismission of the old harbor and of the railway tracks may offer a unique possibility to rethink the urban condition.

Looking from below, via a close reading, a park is a site where we can observe what people of different ages, origins and cultural backgrounds are doing, where and how people meet, stay and rest, looking at other people, showing themselves; where and how they cross the park, coming back to their home, going to the bus stop or to their working places.

Fiumara d'Arte

Location:
Castel di Tusa, Messina,
Italy
Plan: 1982
Implementation: 1982–91
Ordering party:
Antonio Presti
Project team:
Conception: Antonio Presti;
production: various artists
Previous use:
The banks of a river—state-owned land
Current use:
Open-air sculpture park,
art circuit
Surface: 20 ha (49 acres)

Fiumara d'Arte is an open-air sculpture park conceived and promoted by Antonio Presti. It is located on the gravel banks of the river that flows into the sea near Castel di Tusa (Messina).
The project was launched in 1982 with the installation of *La materia poteva non esserci* (There Could Have Been No Matter), a reinforced concrete work by Pietro Consagra. To this eight more artworks were added: Paolo Schiavocampo's *Una curva gettata alle spalle del tempo* (A Curve Cast at the Back of Time) in 1988; Tano Festa's *Finestra sul mare* (Window on the Sea) in 1989; Hidetoshi Nagasawa's *Stanza di barca d'oro* (Gold Boat Room) by the Romei River in 1989; Antonio Di Palma's *Energia mediterranea* (Mediterranean Energy) in 1989; Italo Lanfredini's *Labirinto di Arianna* (Ariadne's Labyrinth) in 1989; Piero Dorazio and Graziano Marini's *Arethusa*, a ceramic decoration adorning the station of the Carabinieri in Castel di Lucio; and *Il muro della ceramica* (The Wall of Ceramics), executed by forty Italian and international artists in 1990.
Presti is installing artworks on state-owned land to express his wish to donate the sculptures to the public. The state thus becomes the rightful owner of the works.
In 1991 Presti inaugurated *Atelier sul mare*, a hotel overlooking the sea at Castel di Tusa. He entrusted the decor of some of its rooms to leading figures from the world of art and culture, such as Mario Ceroli, Luigi Mainolfi, Mauro Staccioli, Fabrizio Plessi, Raoul Ruiz, Pietro Dorazio, Graziano Marini, Michele Canzoneri, Maurizio Mochetti, Paolo Icaro, Dario Bellezza, Hidetoshi Nagasawa, Renato Curcio, Agostino Ferrari, Danielle Mitterand, Cristina Bertelli, Agnese Purgatorio and Maria Lai, who turned these rooms into genuine inhabitable sculptures.
Presti invited the artists to radically alter the function of an ordinary hotel room in such a way as to lend it a different identity: "that of the dream of art."
One of the aims of the Antonio Presti Foundation is to establish a post-graduate study center for the conservation and development of art and architecture within the landscape.
Fiumara d'Arte has thus become an active workshop for ongoing research and a testing ground on both a theoretical and practical level, through an approach based on international dialog.

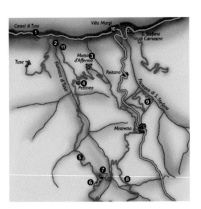

1 Atelier sul mare
2 La materia poteva
  non esserci
3 Energia mediterranea
4 Un chilometro di tela
5 Una curva gettata
  alle spalle del tempo
6 Arethusa
7 Labirinto di Arianna
8 Muro della ceramica
9 Stanza di barca d'oro
10 Finestra sul mare
11 38° Parallelo - Piramide

Riemer Park

Location:
Munich Riem, Bavaria,
Germany
Plan: 1995 (competition)
Implementation:
1997–2005
Ordering party:
Landeshauptstadt
München / MRG GmbH
Project team:
Latitude Nord, landscape
architects, DPLG
Collaborators:
First stage: Gerrit STAHR
and Heinz Haberland;
second stage: LUZ
Landschaftsarchitekten
München
Previous use: Airport
Current use: Public park
Surface:
First stage: 5 ha (12 acres);
second stage: ca 15 ha
(37 acres)
Cost:
First stage:
ca.12.2 million euros;
second stage:
ca. 19 million euros

A park without boundaries: located on the Isar plain, which extends as far as
the alpine foreland, the park is situated on the former site of Munich's airport.
The surrounding landscape is one of contrasting scales and uses (large cultivated
fields, suburban housing and proposed housing developments). The strength
of the project lies in the dramatic interplay between the park and the outstretched
plain. The park's spaces are composed within a planting system which creates
great depth of views, whilst providing for a wide range of uses. A terrace
is situated between the town and the park.

The town of Munich sought an ecologically enduring project, which would follow
the demands of "Agenda 21" directives. The project commenced with a detailed
study of the surrounding environment.

A spatial structure is defined by woodlad masses, groves and hedges.
The orientation and form of these volumes is dictated by the existing built
landscape pattern (farmland, urban development and infrastructure) and by the
prevailing winds. The play on the rhythm and density of planting and topography
is the tool that creates a variety of compositions and spatial perceptions.

The manipulation of the topography pays direct reference to the character
and scale of the Lisard plain. This spatial structure offers the city's inhabitants
the rare luxury of large, accessible and perceptible open spaces.

The circulation network is superimposed on this basic structural pattern. A visitor to
the park can discover a multiplicity of spatial situations, textures and light qualities.
Planting and topography define the open spaces: the plant palette consists
exclusively of native material. Limitless arrangements of patterns are possible.
This dynamism offers varying levels of transparency and depth of views.

The planting and topography facilitate human comprehension of scale and
landscape. The human eye is the means by which we master the perception
of level changes, rhythmic arrangement of light and shadow. The voids are
the true structure of the park.

The plant spacing within these masses creates a range of at first enclosed, and
then increasingly more open, spaces. The plant palette consists of oaks (*Quercus*)
mixed with hornbeams (*Carpinus*) and oaks (*Quercus*) mixed with pines (*Pinus*).
These landmark plantations allow for the perception of a space's depth and scale.
They are part of the structural fluidity within the park. Groves frame views
and magnify the sense of great depth within these views. There are two types,
a large and a small. The former is part of the parks structure: it is aligned along
the east-west axis of the park, and consists exclusively of *Tilia cordata*.

The smaller groupings are freely scattered, always on a north-south axis.
Each individual one is planted exclusively with one species, e.g. *Fraxinus
excelsior*, and consists of between twenty to sixty trees.

Woodland strips create a transparent buffer zone along the park's edges, which reveal the patterns of agricultural use. Specimen or individual trees are incorporated in a variety of ways; as specimens standing alone, arranged in lines or in clusters.

The meadows stretch continuously for 1.5 kilometers. Commencing as grasses on the poorer existing soil of the site, these meadows continue and evolve until becoming moisture loving plantations by the lake shore.

A 180 meter-wide active recreation area acts as a transition zone between town and park, and is the "welcome" gateway to the park. It accommodates the transition between the housing behind and the green spaces beyond. 193 bronze plates adorn the terrace edge.

The hills are landmarks. Being the highest points in the park, as such they offer an overall view of the park and its interaction with the plain beyond. Their location defines the spaces of the east entry and add dramatic emphasis to the lake and the beach.

The swimming lake is a focal point for activity, a meeting place. It also plays a role in protection of the farmland, as it is orientated to guide visitors towards the terrace. Naturally occurring ground water fills the lake.

Natur-Park Schöneberger Südgelände

Location:
Prellerweg 47-49, Berlin,
Germany
Main entrance to the public
transport "Priesterweg"
station (S-Bahn)
Plan: 1986
Implementation:
1996–2009
Ordering party:
Land Berlin: GrünBerlin
Plan and Garten GmbH
Project team:
ARGE Planland/Büro
OkoCon
Collaborators:
Artwork: artist's group
ODIOUS, Berlin; Allianz
Umweltstiftung (Allianz
Environmental Foundation)
Previous use: Railroad
Current use:
Urban public park
Surface:
18 ha (44 acres)
Cost: 3.5 million marks

Located in the so-called "Schöneberger Südgelände" the Tempelhof switch yard was opened in 1889. During the first decades of the 20th century, it became one of the major facilities for railroad freight in Berlin. However, after the Secon World War, due to the developing political situation concerning the city of Berlin, the railway traffic successively declined on this site. In 1952 it was shut down, completely.

During the following decades nature took possession of the terrain and the decaying railroad technique was pushed off to the siding. Spontaneous vegetation spread out over the then "forgotten" area. So a broad diversity of plants, fungi and animals settled here, composed of native species, weed-grown gardening waste from the nearby garden plots, as well as introduced species, obviously remnants of the former Europe-wide train connections. Including several rare and endangered species, they constituted different biocoenoses, such as herbaceous vegetation, dry grassland, ruderal vegetation formed by perennial herbs, and jungle-like woodland.

Owing to successful activities of citizen initiatives in the 1980s and 1990s, the former switch yard was officially declared one of the most precious biocoenoses grown inside the urban vicinity of Berlin; later on, it was even taken under special legal protection (landscape and natural conservation area). After the German reunion in 1990, concepts for the train system were developed for the now unified Capital Berlin. In this new context a Tempelhof switch yard was no longer needed, and therefore, in 1995, the ownership of the area was transferred from the train company to the City of Berlin.

This situation offered the opportunity to preserve this oasis of wilderness, and unfold the ideas of a nature park into reality. Financially supported by the Allianz Environmental Foundation, the area underwent a "soft" development. For example, in order to protect the existing vegetation as much as possible, footpaths were mostly built by filling in soil into the railroad tracks. The highly

sensitive biocoenosis of dry grassland was made accessible by an elevated latticed footbridge, which prevents visitors from stepping off the way into the valuable vegetation. In 2000 the Natur-Park Schöneberger Südgelände was opened to the public. Its size is 18 hectares, about a quarter of which is protected by law ("nature reserve"); most of the rest is under lower protection ("landscape conservation area"). Due to its distinctive features the park was an external project of the Expo 2000.

Within the exuberant vegetation the railroad reminiscences, like tracks, switches, signals, and water cranes are still present, rotting more and more over the years. But together they establish a fascinating mixture of a bygone engineering era and the vigorously vivid nature. Spectacular technical landmarks are the old turntable (originally built in the late 19th century, one of the oldest and still existing ones in Germany), a water tower (built in 1927, an iron construction following the architecture of "New Practicality", about 50 meters high) and a huge hall, built in 1910 (4000 square meters, originally three times larger), where steam locomotives used to be repaired. An outsourced steam engine (series type 50) is another nostalgic attraction in the park.

Besides the railroad remnants and the lush wildlife the third eye-catching "track" in the park is the artwork of the artist's group ODIOUS. So visitors are guided through the nature reserve on a large and "way-pointing" sculpture, the footbridge. Other iron sculptures are fitted into the landscape, as well, or are concentrated in the *giardino segreto*. By using modern means, this draws back to the Italian Renaissance tradition of secrete gardens where a highly structured garden plot was segregated from the surrounding wild-life.

Inside a former administrative building (*Brückenmeisterei*) the park-cafe opens on week-ends during the summer, and several organizations and individuals offer guided tours on various topics. Concerts, various theater performances and other events take place in the *giardino segreto* and the loco-hall.

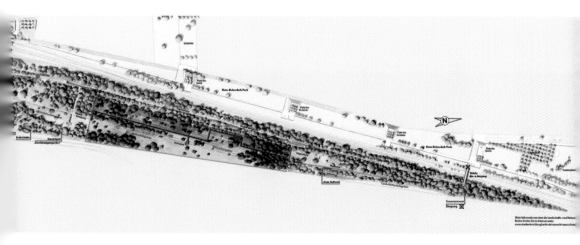

Lagunage de Harnes

Location: Harnes, France
Plan: 1999–2000
Implementation: 2005
Ordering party:
Communauté
d'Agglomeration
Lens-Lievin
Project team:
Agence Paysages
Collaborators:
François-Xavier Mousquet
(landscape designer),
David Verport
Previous use: Mining site
Current use: Water garden
Surface:
17.5 ha (53 acres); 5.5 ha
water basins
Cost: 1.5 million euros

As part of a program to recover industrial wastelands, a nature sewage treatment plant has been created at the lower end of a 25-square-kilometer drainage slope, that manages the liquid residue of some 80,000 inhabitants.

Having excavated the lagoons and canals, the new vegetation was planted directly in the fertile dark slag, residual from the closed coalmines.

To create a frame, three plant species were widely introduced along more than 10 kilometers: honeysuckle (*Lonicera nitida "Maygrün"*), wild cherry (*Cornus sanguinea*) and birch (*Betula verrucosa*).

The watercourses were made watertight with clay.

This aquatic garden of over 7 hectares is a network of lagoons crisscrossed by 3-meter-wide dikes that crate a long route for the water to follow, to complete traditional sewage plant's purifying process and achieve water of safe bathing quality.

Water enters the sewage treatment plant loaded with organic pollution on which the bacteria feed, thereby transforming it into minerals, the load the water carries into the first lagoon.

There, the voracious roots of the willows, planted in a bed of gravel, absorb the maximum amount of manure.

In the second lagoon, the reeds are waiting to absorb the remaining nitrites and phosphates. The rapidly growing vegetable mass is harvested and composted. The attractive flowers and fruit of *Typha angustifolia*, *Butomus umbellatus*, *Iris pseudoacorus* and *Epilobium hirsutum* make these species ecologically and aesthetically interesting. The water reaches the center of the lagoons: to oxygenate it, wind driven pumps throw it 2 meters higher up. It then flows in a thin film down a series of wide concrete steps, receiving ultraviolet

radiation, a traditional disinfection system in Arab countries known as *Chadar* or "veil of water."

The water's journey through the roots will still last two weeks before it reaches the bathing ponds.

A couple of bunkers from the First World War create two islands that are inaccessible to the public. Here birds can nest, and the interior houses a colony of bats.

The area offers a series of short cuts to local schoolchildren, and various sports and leisure activities are practiced, such as running, cycling or strolling.

Informative panels attract the visitor's attention to the sewage treatment process and the animal and plants species that have become observable since it was inaugurated.

Landesgartenschau Eberswalde

Location:
Eberswalde, Brandenburg, Germany
Plan: 1998
(competition, 1st prize)
Implementation:
1998–2002
Ordering party:
Landesgartenschau
Eberswalde 2002 GmbH
Project team:
Topotek 1, Topotek 1
Gesellschaft von
Landschaftsarchitekten
mbH
Collaborators:
Planung Wechselflor:
Isterling & Partner
Previous use:
Industrial site
Current use: Public park
Surface: 17 ha (42 acres)
Cost: 5.5 million euros

Adjacent to the Finow Canal, a former industrial site dating from the early-19th century was cleared and converted into a new type of park. The concept for the transformation of this early industrial area focuses less on heightening the experience of industrial romanticism and more on offering orientation, mapping the site as a post-industrial landscape park. The park contrasts intensive areas of experience with the vastness of space. The uniquely-designed park lavishes details ranging from picturesque situations to urban graphics on a tarmac.

The existing elements of the site were not connected in terms of hierarchy or location, but rather through a dynamic grid. The vast, former industrial site is mapped as a post-industrial park via a system of paths; 40-centimeter-wide steel tapes run through the terrain describing wide radii, most of them accompanied by paths. The steel tapes span the whole of the new park like a geographical map grid of meridians and parallels. They define—and make visible—the expanse of the terrain shaped and re-shaped by the old industrial works over the course of its history.

The elaboration of the spatial potential includes both the accentuation of topographical situations and the interpretive conceptual development of extant elements. For example, the subterranean canals formerly used to cool the rolling mills were opened for pedal boats. This spatial archaeology forms the third component in the multi-faceted cultural landscape of the new park.

A chain of highly-detailed exhibition gardens at the entrance area of the park forms a design-image intended to provide a spatial and thematic contrast to the expanse of the landscape park in the Finow Valley. These densely-concentrated gardens form a conceptual sequel to the 19th-century museum cabinets in which curios were collected for the visitors' amusement. This string of plots is a central element of the garden exhibition and consists of rectangular thematic gardens of approximately 150 square meters. They form showcases for their discrete little worlds with different stagings—a blossoming, odorous, ever-changing collection of garden objects placed in a consciously artificial manner in the park. For example, the "garden of the senses" displays the effect scented plants have on the physical and spiritual well-being of mankind; the medical garden, in which the appropriate healing plants are located at the relevant part of a body represented in silhouette on the ground, conveys physical knowledge. The vital sequence of spaces between the showcases reveals the constantly changing correlation between the gardens during the waxing and waning of the growing season.

Recovery of the Banks of the Rio Gállego

Location:
Zuera, Zaragoza, Spain
Plan: 1999
Implementation: 2000–01
Ordering party:
Zuera Municipality
Project team:
Iñaki Alday, Margarita
Jover, Maria Pilar Sancho
(architects); Conrado
Sancho (civil engineer);
Jorge Abad (biologist);
Corsan-Corviam (builder)
Collaborators:
Montse Escorcell,
Anna Planas, Pablo Alós,
Ma Dolores Sancho
Previous use: Landfill site
Current use:
Public space with
entertainment and leisure
facilities
Surface: 16 ha (40 acres)
Cost:
1.9 million euros material
execution; 2.2 million euros
contracted execution

The project consisted in the sealing of a rubbish dump and the recovery of the space between the Zuera village and the Gállego River, a tributary of the Ebro, as public space. Three needs are the triggers of the landscape and urban recovery; on one hand the security problems of the southern part of the village, attacked perpendicularly by the river, on the other a new connection with the river, so far interrupted by two tailings, and finally, the desire for a permanent bullring.

Aspects of public space: a riverside walk, a park equipped with an amphitheater, two squares and a pedestrian connection between the old town and the river were the main realizations that made open the village to this new space and Gállego River itself. Hydraulic aspects: the improved water quality, protection of the old town, and restoration of the river positively affect the hydraulic system of the site. Ecological aspects: these include the sealing of landfills, the restoration of the green corridor or the riparian forest restoration by cleaning and planting on natural drainage channels of the land, the removal of river border roads and recovery of insularity from the riparian forest and water sanitation driving down to the position of the filter in the project. Aspects of urban planning: they are a new road and two connection squares to the town, management of the newly-built facade, ultimately incorporating the river as an element of urban structure. Interventions are concentrated and austere, as the meager budget (13.70 €/sqm) is used largely in non-visible aspects.

AMD&ART's Vintondale Project

Location:
Vintondale, Cambria
County, Pennsylvania
Plan: 1994
Implementation: 2005
Ordering party:
The community
of Vintondale, Pennsylvania
Project team:
Core design team: T. Allan
Comp (historian and project
director); Bob Deason
(hydrogeologist); Stacy
Levy (sculptor); Julie
Bargmann (landscape
designer)
Collaborators:
Peter Richards,
Angelo Ciotti, Michael
Oppenheimer (sculptors);
Lily Yeh (artist); Claire
Fellman & Emily Neye
(Clean Slate – design
competition winner);
Jessica Gordon Liddell
(Great Map mosaic); Anita
Lucero (mine no. 6 portal
etching)
Previous use: Coal mine
Current use: Public park
Surface: 14 ha (35 acres)
Cost: 1 million dollars

AMD&ART is a small non-profit organization demonstrating that AMD (Acid Mine Drainage) treatment sites, creatively designed *with* the community, have the potential to re-instill a sense of place and pride, allowing community members to forge new connections to the local environment and history. This approach honors a past of hard work and community building, bringing that same civic engagement to the design and construction of treatment systems that cleanse polluted waters, reach people, restore nature and revitalize abandoned spaces. AMD can be either acidic or alkaline, and contains elevated levels of dissolved metals such as iron, aluminum, and manganese. AMD is toxic to aquatic life and often coats streambeds a bright, rusty orange as iron precipitates out of the water. AMD results in both habitat destruction and the loss of waterways as recreational, industrial and community resources. Looming black piles of coal refuse are evidence of the industry's lack of planning and reckless use of resources. Usually hectares in size, and often at a close proximity to community centers, refuse piles take up space that could be developed as public parks, playing fields, shopping centers, and hubs of social and economic activity. Water quality in these regions is grossly impacted by acid mine drainage. AMD&ART, in 1994, in response to these and other environmental problems, began working in and engaging communities at the grassroots level to discuss environmental issues affecting their area… Vintondale, Pennsylvania is one such community. In 1997, AMD&ART and the Borough of Vintondale began working together to initiate a 14-hectare public reclamation park to address one primary AMD discharge. The grassroots commitment of Vintondale residents and the experience of AMD&ART are a potent combination. Vintondale is utilizing AMD&ART's experience to work with the community and translate their ideas into achievable project goals.

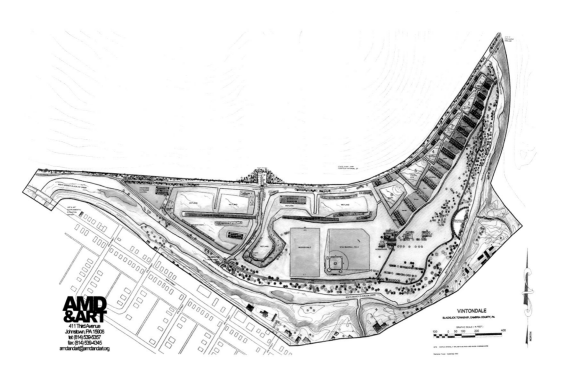

AMD
&ART
411 Third Avenue
Johnstown, PA 15906
tel (814) 539-5357
fax (814) 539-4345
amdandart@amdandart.org

VINTONDALE
BLACKLICK TOWNSHIP, CAMBRIA COUNTY, PA.

Shanghai Houtan Park

Location:
2010 Shanghai Expo Park,
Shanghai, China
Plan: 2005–09
Implementation: 2007–09
Ordering party:
Shanghai 2010
Expo Bureau
Project team:
Turenscape (Beijing Turen
Design Institute): Kongjian
Yu (design principal);
Shihong Lin, Wei Hong,
TianyuanYuan, Hongqian
Yu, Yuan Fang, Yuanyuan
Jin, Xiang Long, Xiangbin
Kong, Dongli Ren,
Yuan Zhang, Haibo Tang,
Weirong Jiang, Yu Qiu,
Shaohui Bai, Meicai, He,
Fan Yang, Junying Zhang,
Yang Pan, Jing Zhang,
Xiangjun Liu, Hongxia Ding,
Jing Niu, Yuan Zhang,
Shaohua Lin, Yanan Zang,
Zongbo Shao, Dehua Liu,
Fumin Yu, Rao Chen,
Wei Zhang, Jiwei Chen,
Xiangrong Wan
Collaborators:
Shanghai Landscape
Construction Company
(construction contractor)
Previous use:
Industrial site
Current use: Public park
Surface:
14 ha (35 acres):
4 ha natural wetland,
10 ha man-made
Cost: 7 million euros

Challenges
The site is a narrow linear 14-hectare band located along the Huangpu River waterfront in Shanghai, China. This brownfield, previously owned by a steel factory and a shipyard, had few industrial structures remaining and the site was largely used as a landfill and lay-down yard for industrial materials and construction debris, both on the surface and buried throughout the site. The water of Huangpu River is highly polluted with a national water quality ranking of Lower Grade V, the worst on a scale of I-V, and is considered unsafe for swimming and recreation and devoid of aquatic life. The eminent site design challenge was to transform this degraded landscape into a safe and pleasant public space.

The existing concrete floodwall was designed to protect against a thousand-year flood event. A conventional retaining wall would continue to limit accessibility and preclude habitat creation along the water's edge, so an alternative flood control design proposal was necessary. The third challenge was the site itself. The objective of the park design was to: create a green Expo, accommodate for a large influx of visitors during the exhibition from May to October, demonstrate green technologies, transform a unique space to make the Expo an unforgettable event, and transition into a permanent public waterfront park after the Expo.

Design strategy: regenerative design and recycled landscape
Regenerative and recycling design strategies used to transform the site into a living system that offer comprehensive ecological services.

Recycled water: constructed wetland and regenerative design
Through the center of the park, a linear constructed wetland, 1.7 kilometers long and 5 to 30 meters wide was designed to create a reinvigorated waterfront as a living machine to treat contaminated water from the Huangpu River. The wetland also acts as a flood protection buffer between the 20- and 1000-year flood control levees. The meandering valley along the wetland creates a series

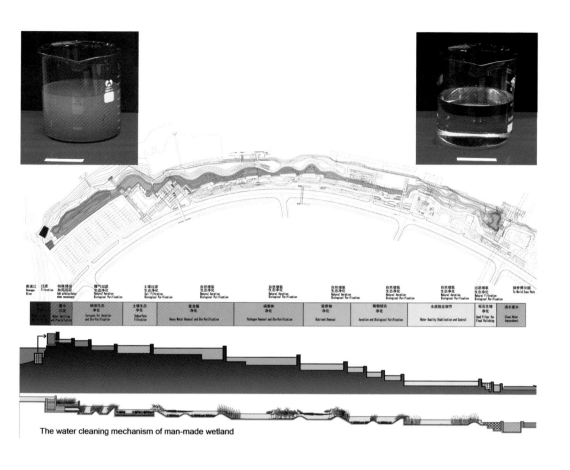

黄浦江 Huangpu River | 过滤 Filtration | 特殊情况加药沉淀 Add precipitator when necessary | 曝气过滤 生态净化 Natural Aeration Biological Purification | 土壤过滤 生态净化 Soil Filtration Biological Purification | 自然增氧 生态净化 Natural Aeration Biological Purification | 自然增氧 生态净化 Natural Aeration Biological Purification | 自然增氧 生态净化 Natural Aeration Biological Purification | 自然增氧 生态净化 Natural Aeration Biological Purification | 自然增氧 生态净化 Natural Aeration Biological Purification | 过滤增氧 生态净化 Natural Filtration Biological Purification | 接世博公园 To World Expo Park

沉砂/沉淀 Water Settling and Precipitation | 梯田生态净化 Terraces for Aeration and Bio-Purification | 土壤生态净化 Subsurface Filtration | 重金属净化 Heavy Metal Removal and Bio-Purification | 病原体净化 Pathogen Removal and Bio-Purification | 营养物净化 Nutrient Removal | 植物综合净化 Aeration and Biological Purification | 水质稳定调节 Water Quality Stabilization and Control | 砂石生物净化 Sand Filter for Final Polishing | 清水蓄水 Clean Water Impoundment

The water cleaning mechanism of man-made wetland

of thresholds offering visual interest and refuge within the bustling world exposition with opportunities for recreation, education, and research.

The re-cycles of seasons
Inspired by the fields of Chinese agricultural landscape, terraces were created to break down the 3–5 meter elevation change from the water's edge to the road, and to slow the runoff directed to the stream in the constructed wetland. The terraces enrich the landscape along the wetland by creating spaces that encourage visitors to enter the living system through the field's corridors and experience the agricultural landscape and wetland firsthand. The paths, like capillaries of a sponge, absorb and pull people to circulate through the park.

Memory: reused industrial structures and materials
Shanghai is the birthplace of industrialization in China and the city witnessed the nation's modern industrial emergence and growth. Factories (only a few structures locate within the site) and cargo piers are the most important industrial structures that remain onsite. The design transformed the existing infrastructure using extraction, infill, and interspersion methods to preserve, reclaim, and recycle them to celebrate the site's industrial past.

The hanging garden: an industrial transformation
The factory building structure located to the south of the Houtan Wetland Park and north of the temporary car park have been reclaimed as a multi-service center—"a hanging garden" hosting a mix of bars and cafes.

Steel panels: an artful installation
An industrial-style installation was constructed using steel panels reclaimed from the site, which is made of a series of folded panels parallel to the stream valley casting shadows and framing views.
The design uses other recycled materials such as old bricks, tiles, and biodegradable bamboo flooring to minimize project costs and to integrate innovative energy efficient technologies into the architecture.

Resilient and transformable strategy
During the Expo, the site demonstrates an ecological city ideology—a productive and healthy urban public green space that focuses on simultaneously addressing pedestrian flows, safety and evacuation routes.

Conclusion
The post-industrial design demonstrates a unique productive landscape evoking the memories of the past and the future of the ecological civilization, paying homage to a new aesthetics based on low carbon ideology, with low maintenance and high performance landscapes.

Crazannes Quarries

Location:
La Pierre de Crazannes
rest area, A837,
Saintes-Rochefort, France
Plan: 1997
Implementation: 1993–97
Ordering party:
Societè des Autoroutes
du Sud de la France (SNCF)
Project team:
Bernard Lassus
Previous use: Stone quarry
Current use:
Motorway rest area
Surface: 12 ha (30 acres)

The parking area La Pierre de Crazannes is an exercise in the reinterpretation of a place and function. The setting is the A837 motorway connecting the city of Saintes to Rochefort-sur-Mer. The site is a former quarry overrun with vegetation and made up of parallel faults of different sizes. It was not selected as a rest area by the Societè des Autoroutes du Sud de la France right from the start (rather, it was conceived as an area to be visited by motorists during their stop), but was only included in the project at a later stage.

The progressive detection of emerging rock surfaces came to shape the very planning of the new motorway landscape. By making careful, gradual inroads into the area, many rocks have been brought to light that bear witness to the existence of the ancient abandoned caves, now overrun by vegetation. The rhythm created by the preservation of the rocks, the outline of their shadows and the depth of the light is what lends the rest area its appearance, ensuring a variety of impressions. Visible faults extend alongside ones on which visitors set their feet, creating a guided itinerary across different faults and vantage points. The most visible green feature in the project is the fern forest that has been preserved: the excavated areas overgrown with plants form an extensive romantic landscape in which the former quarry is linked to the motorway through successive vantage points. The motorist traveling along the road is led to recognize the meaning, the appearance and the memory of the place.

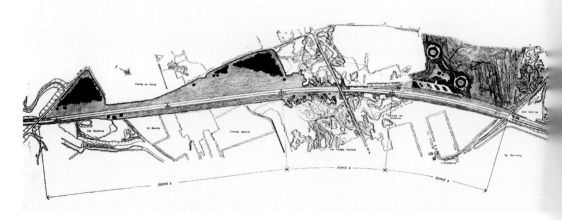

Cultuurpark Westergasfabriek - Amsterdam

Location:
Amsterdam,
The Netherlands
Plan: 1998–2000
Implementation: 2004
Ordering party:
Projectbureau
Westergasfabriek,
Westerpark District Council
& City of Amsterdam
Project team:
Francine Houben
(architect); Arup, Pieters
Bouwtechniek, Tauw
(engineers); *management:*
Northcroft
Previous use:
Industrial site
Current use: Natural park
and cultural center
Surface:
11.5 ha (28 acres)
Costi: 90 million euros

"Changement," Gustafson Porter's competition winning scheme for
the Westergasfabriek, responded to the park's Master Plan by offering diverse
spatial and temporal experiences. The Westergasfabriek is a partially dismantled
19th-century industrial site with vestiges of its layout intact and preserved
in the new concept. The landscape design for the Westergasfabriek park
illustrates in a contemporary form man's changing views and attitude towards
the environment and the resulting landscape types. It also highlights the project's
placement between city and nature.

This project for a new public park on the heavily contaminated site of a former
gas factory presented us with a problem that we could only respond to with
an ecological view. Polluted soil could not be taken offsite to create new problems
elsewhere. So a cut-and-fill balance was calculated, bringing in new soil
to displace polluted soil, retaining existing ground levels around the buildings
and creating a new undulating terrain that was the consequence of surplus soil.
The use of the park is two-fold, a green park environment and a cultural center
with indoor and outdoor activities. A central promenade, the Axis, links the town
hall with the Cité des Arts and a variety of spaces between. The adjacent spaces
give it a varied ambience. A mix of native plants and selected varieties express
a dynamic between human needs and natural order. At the east end
the arrangement of the park reflects the more formal traditional garden type.
The central area reflects the post-war attitude towards landscape as a support

for sports, leisure and recreation. The north-west Overbracker polder reflects the recent past which is representative of a need for a pure nature/ecology approach. The west end reflects current thinking, that environmental harmony must be achieved with man as a participating partner.

In the middlde of the park is the Events Field. A great field slopes into a stone-lined lake, which can be drained for large events and festivals. Reinforced grass allows for the traffic of equipment for concerts and fairs, yet the fields spacious quality and central location make it ideal for family picnics, lazy strolls and casual activities, such as kite-flying, ball games and the energetic games of young children. The lake and amphitheater mound to its north frame the space.

The sculpted amphitheater shields the park from the noise of the railway and provides a south-facing surface on which it is possible to rest whilst watching

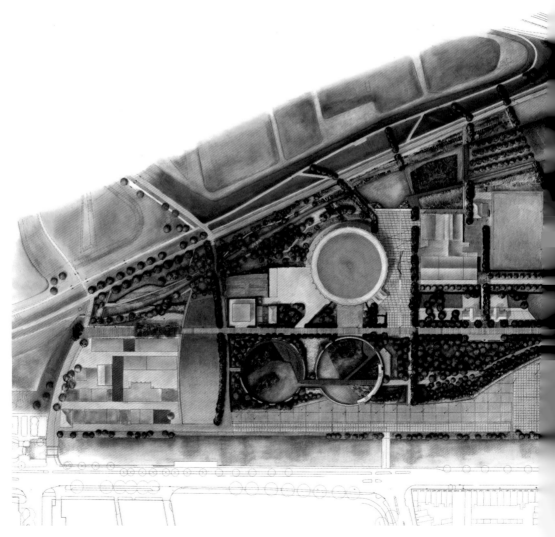

activities on the field below, whilst the proximity of water and stepping-stones in the lake make it a perfect playing area on hot summer days. It the north plaza the park's already existing large trees extend eastwards, and a band of new trees and woodland plants cover a mound that runs the length of the park. Broadway slices a diagonal path through these trees; it passes across the central axis just north of the village, before continuing south-west as far as the circular aquatic and water-lily pools in former gasholders. The type of woodland planting changes in the vicinity of the gasholder pools. New *Salix babylonica* and *Alba tristis* skirt the edge of the remaining basement structures of the gasholders, which have been filled with polluting waste and capped to become a contemplative water-lily pool and verdant aquatic garden, in which floating timber walkways and terraces have been inserted.

10 ha

New Landscapes: Operations of Selection
Michela De Poli

Landscape planning is a practice of study, investigation and interpretation; a process of measured action within a network of connections of various nature—between people, objects, functions, and forms of organization. Working with and for the landscape means exploring the different ways in which it presents itself and operating selections.

"On countless occasions we walk through the wilderness and perceive, with the most diverse levels of attention, trees and water, meadows and wheat fields, hills and houses, and the thousands of changes in the light and the clouds, yet because we pay attention to one thing in particular, and although we may also see this and that together, we are still not aware of seeing a 'landscape.' [...] Nature, which in its deep essence and meaning ignores individuality, is transformed into the individuality of the 'landscape' by man's gaze, which divides things and then configures what it has divided as distinct units."[1]

In order to interpret a landscape, one must adopt a multi-scale approach, in such a way as to be capable of focusing on each of the various objects of attention. The interpretation of the landscape constitutes a field for multidisciplinary interrelations.

The landscape is a complex organism consisting of visible parts, which may be interpreted in terms of forms, and less visible parts, which consist of systems of relations. The landscape, as it has been codified, represents—i.e. shows and presents—the outcome of a transcription based on actions produced by man with various degrees of awareness. Each alteration of the living body of a territory has immediate repercussions, which occur within a short distance of time and space, as well as—at a subsequent stage—long-term consequences, which only gradually manifest themselves and are spatially removed.

Every observation engenders a selection, opens a window in the broad territorial system, and marks out given sections of the landscape through a personal interpretation: "What we encompass with our gaze or within our temporary horizon is not a landscape yet, but rather material for it—just as a pile of books is not 'a library,' but will become it, without having to add or remove anything, once a unifying concept orders them according to its own formal concept."[2] The vision we derive by looking at places stems from a dynamic combination organized by the eye and mind, which combines recognizable parts with mental processes, adding to what is visible what our cultural background enables us to conceptualize. What we see, what appears around us, is the outcome of a process of assimilation that enables us to perceptually "operate" on a finished product which is the result of endless co-presences and co-responsibilities but is "temporarily" closed: the visualization of an image that is provisionally final because it is in constant motion.

The process of selection does not merely yield images; rather, it lends the project its active value, as the conscious action of controlled alterations and careful transformations: through programs based on combined selections, landscapes are restored—degraded, uncertain and abandoned landscapes,[3] ones apparently isolated from a rhythm and time that has cut them off.

Selection shapes the final outcome—and this applies to the landscape as much as to all complex production structures in which a given material is manufactured by bringing discarded pieces back into circulation. In the past, steel used to be obtained by mining (with all that this practice entails); nowadays it is obtained from ferrous waste of various origin, metal that is discarded after having served various uses and functions.

This is a cultural operation, since in most cases waste is not a material condition but an interpretative/subjective one;[4] as such, it is subject to being altered: its identity is given by the difficulty of identifying it and the possibility of framing it within standard categories through which it may be made the most of as a "common good."

Abandonment may concern a "container" and/or its "content"; spaces, *terrains vagues*, or volumes. It affects people and shapes communities. Ultimately, it leaves scars on the individuals who over time have experienced those spaces and functions.

In each of these expressions, the object of abandonment has lost its codified connections, those determined by its pre-established function. It comes across as powerless, useless, and removed from reality and functionality. Actually, once a space, area or building is abandoned and apparently ignored, it establishes new links with the surrounding landscape: new relations and qualities that are so charged as to become potentially dominant and prevalent compared to its recent past.

More so than other sites, degraded sites are heterogeneous structures, dormant ones that enclose manifold potential meanings and contrasting temporal complexities, stemming from different interruptions—conscious or sudden interruptions, prearranged or imposed ones. Degraded landscapes are bodies out of control both within, where their functionality has been erased, and without, in their exterior relations, where the natural elements from a third landscape lead to a spontaneous reintegration with the environment.

New urban natures, strategic urban natural forms, are sprouting up all around us, for us to examine and interpret them—even though they are capable of gradually evolving on their own and of blending with other "abandoned" natural forms.

Within a context of this sort some things are not easy to identify; our contribution to the identification of new landscapes lies in understanding what may endure. Deciding what may remain in a place altered by its defunctionalization and by the lack of human management means understanding how to interpret the transformation of a landscape—as we operate according to a given, measurable time frame, as points of transition within the newly acquired time scale—and for how long it will remain a "marker" of endurance.

This might be described as a kind of "waste sorting" that is carried out not by the archeologist but by the rubbish man, who distinguishes, separates, divides and gathers what is still useful among existing residues.

The plan to reintroduce such things within a territory requires a strategy of selection with regard to time, memory, form, matter and all those other elements that once rearranged can set a discarded residue within a different landscape.

It is not a matter of searching for fragments to be recomposed as archeological remains arranged according to their original layout, or of bringing to life what is dead and buried. This is rather an opportunity to bestow a new life and time on things. The archeologist restores and recreates those components which recall the previous existence of an object by placing the latter outside time and space—since its original time and place have changed. The archeological substance of the item is where its value lies, and its relation to time is always a relation to past time.

The planning of degraded landscapes instead introduced a new time, because vestiges gather too much history to express a history of their own[5] and must be set within a new rhythm in order to come back to life.

As already noted, the body that is operated upon is not an utterly passive one; rather, it is precisely by grasping the value of its uncertain state that the work takes shape, based on a form of continuity that through transformation enables the transition from one life to another without the need for the former to die first. This selection expresses man's capacity to regenerate himself through an almost primordial, visceral effort; a powerful effort that is capable of controlling the landscape by means of specialized, multi-disciplinary and wide-ranging knowledge. If this is defused, however, it will only extend the death-throes and produce not a dead body but a monstrous one.

The selection of what endures must occur as in the process of film editin, where a breakdown produces individual frames that then appear during viewing as an integrated flow of different components; the arrangement of the frames, whatever the criteria governing it, engenders an overall image stemming from selections and cuts operated for the sake of the narrative—as in the process of photography, which exploits the principle that every shade of color can be reproduced through the superimposition of primary colors.

In all these analogies, it is clear that selection does not require any particular scale or size. The *Atlas*, with its choice of projects—reclaimed plots of land and quarries, former rubbish dumps and *terrains vagues*—illustrates opportunities for regeneration ranging from broad territorial projects to domestic experiments. Planning creates new conditions by manipulating altered spaces, exploited areas and impoverished settings, ensuring a new social, economic and environmental prosperity. The communities involved were all marked, at varying degrees, by a state of degradation. The *Atlas* emphasizes the importance of focusing on specific places through projects that find their raison d'etre in the future possibility of appreciating their process of creation of new landscapes.

The common denominator is the development of sites through reinterpretations that only in some cases seek to replace the existing content of a container, but which in most cases explore sensible notions such as those of matter, state, place and community, operating on the basis of spatial qualities that are evident because of their degree of reactivity. In such a way, passive environments are turned into collective resources: the chief value of extreme settings in which the critical acknowledgement of one quality of an abandoned, rejected space—as in the case of the Líthica quarries in the Balearic Islands—makes it possible to save the site from demolition.

If we accept the definition of "non-place," then there are no "annihilated," erased places that are lost once and for all—only places that require a considerable rehabilitation time. This is illustrated, for instance, by the project for the Kam Kotia mine in Ontario, which focused on a sealed-off, contaminated site through repeated attempts at reactivation. The state of abandonment of the place only added to the distress affecting an increasingly large environment area, until a plan for the regeneration and reclaiming of these 200 hectares of land was developed. The same applies to forgotten areas, in which a "nature" out of control takes over and defines spaces that then become exceptions to be safeguarded within a dense urban fabric. This has been the case, in particular, with the former 18-hectare railway site in Berlin that is now protected as a "nature reserve": the public *Natur-Park Schöneberger Südgelände*. Here the work undertaken by man is one of conservation and consolidation.

The projects reflect cultural operations which bear witness to an ethical commitment, a desire for reinterpretation, a shared focus, and an innovative mode of planning. One is reminded of the operative approach to the destruction of books adopted by the silent Hant'a, the protagonist of Bohumil Hrabal's tale,[6] a man who has been working at a mechanical press for thirty-five years. In his solitude, he recomposes the shredded paper to form wonderful colored parallelepipeds, each enclosing an outstanding author. Each parcel to be shredded contains a valuable volume—with authors ranging from Goethe to Kant and Nietzsche. But inside the crushed material, each work is preserved whole, thanks to a particular method devised by Hant'a himself. This methodical work of assigning "value" to each paper monolith betrays an innovative effort to "create beauty"[7] and assemble a parcel he won't have to be ashamed of.

[1] G. Simmel, "Filosofia del paesaggio," in M. Sassatelli (ed.), *Saggi sul paesaggio*, Armando editore, Rome 2006.
[2] *Idem.*
[3] "'Landscape' means an area, as perceived by people, whose character is the result of the action and interaction of natural and/or human factors. [...] It includes land, inland water and marine areas. It concerns landscapes that might be considered outstanding as well as everyday or degraded landscapes." *European Landscape Convention* – Florence, 20 October 2000.
[4] T. Griffero, *Atmosferologia. Estetica degli spazi emozionali*, Editori Laterza, Rome-Bari 2010. "The aesthetic identity of a landscape may thus coincide with the atmosphere we perceive within it, for the most part in a half-unconscious way: a kind of psyco-physical condition, like a constant bass note, that accompanies our existence and influences it."
[5] M. Augè, *Che fine ha fatto il futuro? Dai nonluoghi al nontempo*, Elèuthera, Milan 2009.
[6] B. Hrabal, *Too Loud a Solitude*, Harcourt Brace Jovanovich, San Diego 1990.
[7] *Idem.*

Gas Works Park

Location:
Seattle, Washington
Plan: 1971
Implementation: 1973–75
Ordering party:
Seattle Department
of Parks and Recreation
Project team:
Richard Haag Associates
with Douglas Tuma,
Stephen G. Ray,
Kenichi Nakano
Collaborators:
Olson Walker and
Associates (architects);
Michael G. Ainsley
(lavatory/concession
building architect with
Richard Haag Associates);
Richard Brooks
(bioremediation consultant)
Previous use: Gas plant
Current use: Public park
Surface: 8 ha (20 acres)
Cost: 2 million dollars

"Manufactured gas was perhaps the single most important industrial enterprise of the 19th century, 160 years of technical achievement. Gas turned night into day, inquiring minds were enlightened in the public library system, factories worked night shifts and America's GNP exceeded Great Britain's in our Centennial Year (1876). In the USA alone, more than 3500 'town' gas plants existed. The Lake Station (aka Seattle Gas Plant) became Seattle's 'central station' and replaced three earlier plants. It operated from 1906 to 1956, after which natural gas was distributed through the same underground pressurized network. Gas Works Park in Seattle features the most complete assemblage of gas-manufacturing 'sets', gas conditioning and machinery in the world; only remnant elements of this great and rampant industry remain elsewhere."[1]
"Gas Works Park, modest in means and radical in effect, shatters an almost universal attitude of how a park should look and what it might be."[2]
It came to be the first industrial reclamation park in the world, pioneering recycling of obsolete structures and bioremediation of the terrain vague.
After thirteen years of abandonment, Richard Haag, a landscape architect, was commissioned to analyze the 8-hectare site to determine if it could be possible to create a public park on the ruins. After lengthy sojourns to the site including overnight camping, a sensitivity to the "bones," the brutality, the ghostly relics began to grow—new eyes for old. This gothic genius loci was way different—no topography, no native soil, no trees, no vegetation, no streams, no stonecrops. The most sacred element was the "Mother" tower close to the lake. An early pledge was made to save her, but the cracking towers were a family, best to show respect.
Slowly the idea of preservation, with the promise of future adaptive use evolved. The first public reaction to this suggestion was outrage. The generational memory of the down-winders was total demolition, seal the site with asphalt, and build athletic courts. RHA began a two-year educational campaign to expand

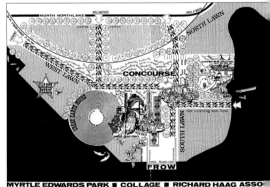

MYRTLE EDWARDS PARK ■ COLLAGE ■ RICHARD HAAG ASSO

and elevate the consciousness of the community to new possibilities.

The first big move was to recycle the grungy blacksmith shop into a bright cheerful research and design office open to the public. Nothing teaches better than demonstration. The second big move was to prove that the gas plant owner could save 100,000 dollars by saving selected structures. The city waived total demolition. The caveat was that features could always be removed but never be replaced. The third big move was to prove that bioremediation would be a natural and cheap way to reduce hydrocarbon infusions to acceptable levels, the clean and green concept.

The site specific microbial communities that depend on oil-based molecules (evolved through six decades) lay dormant. On-site demonstration plots proved that aeration (deep tilling of waste sawdust and sewage sludge) activated the bacteria. The success of this low cost/low technology experiment ensured the park could be built and the idea that "nature can heal itself" is now promoted by regulatory agencies as "land farming."

Ironically, soot infused condensation corroded the steel buildings but preserved the great wooden sheds. The exhauster structure was imagineered as the Playbarn, the boiler building, the Picnic Shed. Adaptive use ensured unmatched experiences on unique machinery at huge savings, new math. The same recycling strategy sculpted the level barren land into a sequence of earth forms climaxing in kite hill, its prominence is to the lake community as Mount Rainier is to the region.

Friends of Gas Works Park, a citizen's coalition formed in 1995, have obtained Historic Landmark Preservation Status from the City of Seattle and the State of Washington.

[1] Allen W. Hatheway, geological engineer.
[2] Laurie Olin, landscape architect.

The Garden of Energies, Experimental Garden

Location:
Cattenom, Moselle, France
Plan: 2004
(competition, 1st prize)
Implementation:
2004–in progress
Ordering party:
Community of the
Communes of Cattenom
and surrounding areas
Project team:
Pascal Cribier
Collaborators:
Francis Hallè (professor
of Tropical Botanics),
Jean-Marie David
(agricultural engineer),
Jean Mahot (horticultural
engineer), Alain Cardon
(architect); *technical studies
office:* Est ingénierie;
Monique Mosser
(art historian and engineer
at the CNRS)
Previous use:
Nuclear plant
Current use:
Experimental energy garden
Surface: 8 ha (20 acres)
Cost: 1.8 million euros

First you need to embark. Going on board already means penetrating the landscape that opens up before your eyes: a lake the extension of which approaches and merges with that of the horizon. […] The boat sets course for an island… The island… This stretch of land with a luxurious vegetation in the middle of the lake is calculated to astonish and teach visitors […] Extending alongside the large grassy avenue is a perforated concrete walkway that enables visitors to make their way into the green, while avoiding any "showcase effect": visitors are free to explore all areas of the park. The sinuousness of the paths is not gratuitous, but reflects this idea of exploration. […] The range of inclinations and orientations makes it possible to play on contrasts, creating rather significant variations in the living conditions of the plants, in such a way as to bring out a number of phenomena.
(*from the competition report*)

Modular greenhouses, anti-freeze tunnels, and natural areas
The layout of the garden, in line with its underlying spirit, stresses the juxtaposition of different strategies and breaks free from the "themed garden effect"[…].
At the center of each scientific area, heated glasshouses house rare or particularly valuable tropical plants. These glasshouses are linked by removable anti-freeze tunnels […] The rest of the planted surface enjoys the natural local climate. Within each thematic sector three areas with different temperatures set plants from almost opposite climates in contrast. This arrangement perfectly illustrates the behavior and functioning of plants in relation to the three fundamental factors that govern all gardens: light, water, and the composition of the soil.

The meadow
At the end of an educational journey to the summit of the island, a new landscape opens up before the visitor's eyes. This is the entrance to the Meadow of the Winds: three separate and independent oval bases appear […] The plant installed 12 meters above the level of the lake requires a pumping system to ensure the raising of the waters. Aside from illustrating the need for electric energy to oppose the force of gravity, this system highlights the presence of the nuclear plant, without which the garden would never benefit from so much technology—indeed, would not exist at all […].
The smokestacks rise beyond the treetops towards the western tip. Enveloped by downy vapors, they affirm their role as the creators of this garden, while remaining elusively distant […].
The dominant theme of this area, however, is wind energy. The phenomenon of anamorphosis is illustrated—the way in which plants adapt to the wind, endure it and are deformed by it—as is that of anemochory, namely the dispersal of seeds or pollen by the winds. This idea is further emphasized by means of an amusing experimental infrastructure, the Corridor of the Winds: two parallel walls cut across the area, in such a way that the breeze it channels gains momentum and leaves its mark on the plants.

The cave
Just as visitors get the impression that their tour of the island is over, they meet an underground passage. [...] This is a corridor extending for 100 meters or so. This space, which magnetically draws visitors, is dotted with the light reflected by countless narrow wells. Each halo of light corresponds to a column overgrown with plants specifically fond of the shade, if not darkness. Herein lies the *raison d'être* of this place: in the creation of an environment dark enough to enable the growth of plants which do not like much light [...] This area shows how "cave-dwelling" species react to such extreme conditions and illustrates their energy-saving strategies. Visitors can discover the opposite of this world on the top surface of the cave: the plants here are in full sunlight and receive little water. Just as the nuclear plant seeks to feed back into the Moselle water "identical to that it has drawn" [...] the garden aims to support it in this goal. It therefore pursues a well-defined objective: lowering the temperature of the water passing through the island by a few degrees.

Promenade Plantée

Location: Place
de la Bastille-Bois
de Vincennes, Paris, France
Plan: 1984
Implementation:
1987–2000
Ordering party:
Municipality of Paris
Project team:
Jacque Vergely, Patrick
Berger, Philippe Mathieux,
Andreas Christo-Foroux,
Vladimir Mitrofanoff,
Roland Schweitzer,
and Pierre Colboc
Previous use: Railroad
Current use: Public park
Surface: 6.5 ha (16 acres),
4.7 km (2.9 miles)

The old railway line—the long track leading from the center of Paris to
La Varenne-Saint-Maur which was inaugurated in 1859 and closed in 1969—has
been reconfigured as a public space, a *coulée verte* extending across the city.
The project turns the old 4.7-kilometer-long railway line into a green stretch linking
Place de la Bastille with the Bois de Vincennes.
In 1988 the linear strip which had long divided the local territory was turned
into a connecting element and point of contact between two sides of the city—
abandoned or poorly developed areas. The new landscape that has emerged
brings together all the distinguishing features of the railway line, which were
redeveloped to create a strip park whose layout provides unusual visual
and physical points of contacts with the city. The process of disassembly
and reassembly extends above the railway level, connecting different surface
areas through stairways and terraces. The rigid track cuts across Paris like
a furrow running between its buildings. The path unfolds across bridges, tunnels
and viaducts, as the gutted railway line turns into a seamless green channel.
The promenade is subdivided into two sections: the first, known as Viaduc des Art,
consists in a 9-meter-long garden that includes almost 200 different plant species;
the second, known as Promenade Verte, is a straight path running below the street
level and obtained through the restoration of a railway tunnel. Here the
spontaneous, wild vegetation has been preserved and new plants have been added.
The strip park is punctuated by themed gardens: the Jardin Hector-Mallot,
Jardine de Reully, Jardin de la Gare de Reully, and Jardin Charles Pègury.

High Line

Location:
New York
Plan: 2003 (competition)
Implementation: 2009–11
Ordering party:
City of New York
Project team:
Diller Scofidio + Renfro: Elizabeth Diller, Ricardo Scofidio, Charles Renfro (partners); Matthew Johnson (project designer); Robert Condon, Tobias Hegemann, Gaspar Libedinsky, Jeremy Linzee, Miles Nelligan, Dan Sakai (project team). James Corner Field Operations (project lead): James Corner (principal-in-charge); Lisa Tziona Switkin, Nahyun Hwang (lead project designers); *project team:* Sierra Bainbridge, Tom Jost, Danilo Martic, Tatiana von Preussen, Maura Rockcastle, Tom Ryan, Lara Shihab-Eldin, Heeyeun Yoon, Hong Zhou; *technical specifications:* Paul DiBona Specifications LLC

Inspired by the melancholic, unruly beauty of the High Line, where nature has reclaimed a once-vital piece of urban infrastructure, the project team retools this industrial conveyance into a post-industrial instrument of leisure, life, and growth. By changing the rules of engagement between plant life and pedestrians, the strategy of "agri-tecture" combines organic and building materials into a blend of changing proportions that accommodates the wild, the cultivated, the intimate, and the hyper-social. In stark contrast to the speed of Hudson River Park, this parallel linear experience is marked by slowness, distraction and an other-worldliness that preserves the strange character of the High Line. Providing flexibility and responsiveness to the changing needs, opportunities, and desires of the dynamic context, the team's proposal is designed to remain perpetually unfinished, sustaining emergent growth and change over time.

Collaborators:
Buro Happold:
*Structural/MEP
engineering:*
Craig Schwitter (principal);
Herbert Browne, Dennis
Burton, Andrew Coats,
Anthony Curiale, Mark
Dawson, Beth Macri, Sean
O'Neill, Stan Wojnowski,
Zac Braun, David Bentley,
Elizabeth Devendorf, Alan
Jackson, Christian Forero,
Joseph Vassilatos.
Robert Silman Associates:
*structural
engineering/historic
preservation:*
Joseph Tortorella, Andre
Georges; *planting design:*
Piet Oudolf; *lighting design:*
L'Observatoire
International; Hervé
Descottes, Annette
Goderbauer, Jeff Beck
Previous use: Railroad
Current use: Public park
Surface: Length 2.4 km
(1.5 miles)
Cost: 152.3 million dollars

Parco Lineare

Location:
Caltagirone
and Piazza Armerina,
Catania, Italy
Plan: 1998–99
Implementation: 2001
Ordering party:
Municipality of Caltagirone
(Catania) and Municipality
of San Michele di Ganzaria
(Catania)
Project team:
Marco Navarra
and Giovanni Branciforti
Collaborators:
A. Messina, M.G. Marino,
S. Gozzo, D. Diana,
and S. Capezzi
Previous use: Railroad
Current use: Public park
Surface: length 14 km
(9 miles)
Cost: 1.5 million euros

The strip park between Caltagirone and Piazza Armerina
The project is part of a more general plan to redevelop the narrow-gauge railway
that used to connect Caltagirone with Piazza Armerina and Dittaino, across
the territories of San Michele di Ganzaria and Mirabella Imbaccari. This railway,
built in the 1920s and 1930s, only remained in use for forty-odd years, up until
1971. The challenges posed by the orography and landscape features, particularly
along the Caltagirone-San Michele di Ganzaria stretch, required the construction
of considerable—and for those times rather bold—engineering feats (galleries,
bridges and viaducts).
The railway used to run across the original landscape like a furrow or scar. It abided
by its own rules and principles, corresponding to the requirements posed by
machines in motion. Its construction thus unfolded through a well-ordered alternation
of excavations and fillings, as may still be seen by walking along the remaining track,
with its syncopated rhythm of areas open or closed to the landscape.
The project more specifically concerns the disclosure of ancient agricultural,
natural and historical landscapes in a region of Sicily on the border between
the Erean and Hyblaean Mountains through the establishment of a new vantage
point. The project aims to set up a light infrastructure through the redevelopment
of works that, while abandoned, in various ways represent a permanent
and well-defined feature of the landscape, having survived its violent
transformation over the last thirty years.
Given the value of these local resources, it is clear that the more general aim
of the project is not merely to restore them, but to carry out a more subtle
and complex operation consisting in the re-establishment of those invisible links
between landscapes, man-made structures, remains and history that might

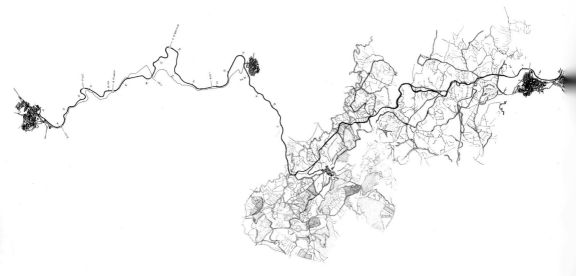

inspire a broader renovation of resources currently not in use (rural buildings, monuments, environmental assets and landscapes). In this respect, the redevelopment of the railway line as a cycle or horse path (or a path for hiking, jogging or skating) and strip park represents a crucial operation for reconstructing an abandoned structure.

This nature trail is conceived as a newly designed light structure which joins a strip park developed from the railway line. It consists in rows of cypresses and dense plots of different shrubs planted along the slopes of the embankments and cuttings. The project engages with the theme of the landscape by constantly entwining two different levels: the material construction of the park (the rows of plants, surfaces, gardens, colors, smells, etc.) and the construction of different ways of viewing and recognizing agricultural and natural landscapes through a variety of principles and tools—both classic ones, such as frames and the line of the horizon, and contemporary ones, such as sequences, assemblages and a range of images. This is ensured by the installation of objects of various sizes along the trail, conceived as recurrent, recognizable elements.

An overall strategy has thus been developed that is based on the possibility of carrying out different operations across an extended period of time, with specific materials and in specific ways. These materials have been arranged as lines, points and surfaces, while the operations planned for the future range from the upkeep and refurbishment of the new structure to its careful reintegration.

The project has taken the form of an ordering of different lines, with different meanings and directions. These lines dynamically run across various points and surfaces, turning landscapes into aesthetic, economic and social energy fields.

Old Airfield Kalbach / Bonames

Location:
Bonames, Frankfurt
am Main, Germany
Plan: 2002–03
Implementation: 2003–04
Ordering party:
Grunflachenomt frankfurt
am Main
Project team:
GTL Gnüchtel -
Triebswetter Landscape
Architecture:
Markus Gnüchtel, Roland
Nagies, Klaus W. Rose
Collaborators:
GrünGürtel by
Environmental Agency,
Frankfurt am Main
Previous use: Army airfield
Current use: Public park
Surface: 7.7 ha (19 acres)
Cost: 1.3 million euros

After closing down the former US Army helicopter airfield, Bonames seemed to stay behind as a relic of the cold war like a contaminant in the near-natural floodplains of the Nidda River.

The Nidda River itself is currently canalized and restrained by weirs in this area, and in wide course sections. The paths on the right and on the left of the Nidda River and the river surrounding represent an extremely popular recreation area in Frankfurt, which leads into the landscape of this region or into the Rhine-Main regional park.

The area is specifically protected as a part of the landscape conservation area II, and of the green belt area. It is located in the legally determined flood plain of the Nidda River, and in the immediate vicinity of the Riedwiesen nature reserve.

The basic idea behind the design is to modify the original airfield and its materiality so gently that the military character of the area melts into the surrounding nature to produce a new unity. Simultaneously, the former airfield was opened to the public for recreational outdoor uses.

The design realization started with a compromise (in the interest of nature protection). Three of the 4.5 hectares of sealed total area were unsealed, 50% of the tar-polluted areas (tree copse, 1/3 of the runway; 7500 tons) were broken off, fractionated and built in again in separately selected grain sizes, varying from 10 square meter concrete clods down to fine gravel, thus creating a wide amplitude of habitat conditions, like moisture and proliferation of nutrients. The remaining 1.5 hectares now serve as a playground and circulation space.

The buildings remained, apart from two. It would have been anachronistic to recreate the old floodplain meadows. And, on top of that, large amounts of waste ground would have had to be moved to the landfills.

Thus a series of succession processes of ever changing plant and animal societies is started, giving a fulminant show of nature's reconquering powers also to non-botanists. Starting from a desert-like status at the beginning to a supposed climax forest in the end, the former airfield exhibits its ecological potential to those visitors using the remaining 50% of the hardscape. This hardscape is meant to be used for all kinds of outdoor activities like roller-skating, cycling or just picnicking.

The biological processes are subject to long term research that will study and document the development of the different plant societies.

Being awarded with the German Award for Landscape Architecture, the design for the airport offers a new approach to the creation of a public park. Given a difficult plot of land with vast areas to be demolished and deposited at high cost, the strategy of keeping the whole quantity of concrete waste within the area gives way to a most unconventional, sustainable park with minimal future maintenance costs, not to forget the construction costs, which were very reasonable. The somewhat contradictory demands of environmentalists on one hand and the wishes of the local residents on the other hand even helped bring the design to a new level of complexity.

Maurice Rose Airfield stands for an extraordinary conversion of a surface formerly used by the armed forces. The history of its military use can still be experienced. The concrete and asphalt relics will generate an interesting plant mosaic. The grounds were incorporated into Frankfurt's green belt.

Park de Hoge Weide

Location:
Leidsche Rijn, Utrecht,
The Netherlands
Plan: 1998–2002
Implementation:
1999–2005
Ordering party:
Projectbureau Leidsche Rijn
Project team:
Sylvia Karres, Bart Brands,
Marie-Laure Hoedemakers,
Joost de Natris, Annette
van Straten, Jim Navarro,
Craig Douglas, Rudolf
Zielinski
Previous use: Landfill site
Current use:
Archaeological park
Surface: 6 ha (15 acres)
Cost: 1.3 million euros

The Leidsche Rijn district on the outskirts of Utrecht is the largest outer city housing development area in the Netherlands, but it is too regimented and too predictable. Children today grow up in anonymous neighborhoods like these without any space for adventure. The design and implementation process for Park de Hoge Weide breaks away from this tendency.
It is not a standard off-the-peg park, but a slowly developing area with sufficient space for experiment and reflection, reacting in a concrete way to participation and (re-)use.
The location, an old landfill site that functions as a soil depot for the whole Leidsche Rijn district, provides the initial foundations for the design. A spatial network of crossing and overlapping dykes is created with soil originating from the depot. The variations in ground level formed in this way offer maximum opportunities for further development, detailing and usage. Recycled building materials are used for paths, steps, bridges or other elements. The park is opened to the public during construction, inviting the users to create new forms of usage. The park grows over time together with its surroundings, and reacts to its users. Not "closed due to construction work," but "open for construction work"!
This process, where design, construction, use and management occur simultaneously, turned out to be difficult to sustain over time in a tradition municipal organizational structure. The development of the park was halted, to the great dissatisfaction of local residents and the designers.
Political pressure ultimately led to a new design commission with new specifications.

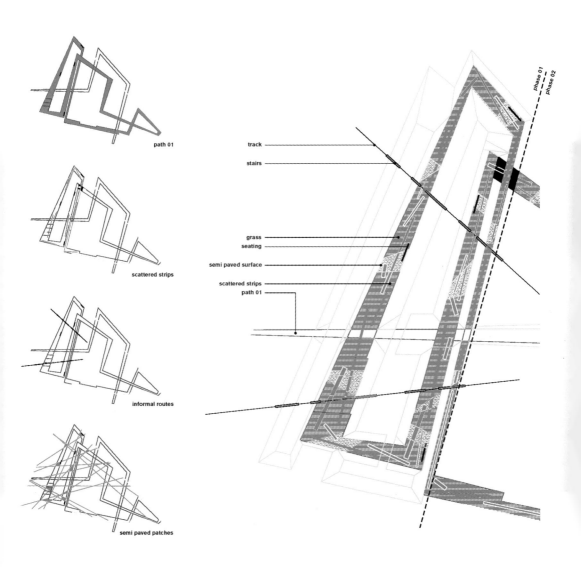

path 01

scattered strips

informal routes

semi paved patches

track

stairs

grass

seating

semi paved surface

scattered strips

path 01

phase 01

phase 02

Northside Park

Location:
Denver, Colorado
Plan: 2000
Implementation: 2002
Ordering party:
City and County of Denver;
Parks Department
Project team:
Wenk Associates:
William Wenk, FASLA, RLA
Principal / Billy Gregg
(project manager)
Previous use:
Industrial site
Current use: Public park
Surface: 5.7 ha (14 acres)
Cost: 4.1 million dollars

Northside Park is located on the South Platte River within a short walk
of the Globeville and Swansea neighborhoods of industrial north Denver.
Several years ago, the Northside Park site was severely blighted. It contained
the vandalized and graffiti-covered remains of a 1930s sewage-treatment plant
that had been closed for thirty years.
The creation of the park grew out of an environmental settlement. In 1987,
a group of Globeville citizens sued the American Smelting and Refining Company
(ASARCO) for contaminating the area's soils with airborne lead from a nearby
smelter. The 1 million dollar settlement was applied to the 4.1 million cost
of cleaning up this Superfund site in preparation for building Northside Park.
Completely razing the site was cost prohibitive. However, recycling components
saved 30% over initial demolition estimates, making the park a reality.
Wenk Associates completed planning through construction of Northside Park
through "design by subtraction." By saving elements of the plant's foundations
and infrastructure, Wenk Associates created functional urban sculpture in a park.
Foundational sections from the treatment plant's clarifying tanks were redefined
as seating walls for youth soccer fields. A concrete-lined drainage channel was
re-routed to create wetlands that improve water quality and add to the richness
of the park environment. Nearly 27 kilometers of the plant's concrete was crushed
and used as fill to create areas for open play and a kite-flying hill. Rebar
was recycled at a plant within view of Northside Park. About 53,000 cubic meters
of earth were moved. A wildlife viewing blind was created from recycled
Stapleton Airport runway concrete. A stretch of the South Platte River
was re-graded and planted with native species. The river has returned
to a more natural state brimming with wildlife.
Northside Park has generated international attention. The project has won
the ASLA Merit Award for Design and the EPA Region 8 Phoenix Award
for Excellence in Brownfields Redevelopment. It is a shining example
of "Recycling in the landscape."

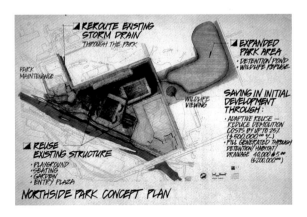

Alumnae Valley at Wellesley College

Location:
Wellesley, Massachusetts
Plan: 2001
Implementation: 2005
Ordering party:
Wellesley College
Project team:
MVVA, Michael Van
Valkenburgh Associates
Collaborators:
Civil engineering:
Vanasse Hangen Brustlin
(Watertown, MA);
electronics engineering:
ARUP (Cambridge, MA);
geotechnical engineering:
Haley and Aldrich (Boston,
MA): *surveys:*
R.E. Cameron and
Associates (Norwood, MA);
soil scientist: Pine and
Swallow Environmental
(Groton, MA);
meadow consultant:
Prairie Restoration
(Princeton, MN);
irrigation systems: Irrigation
Management and Services
(Natick, MA)
Previous use:
Toxic waste landfill site
Current use:
College campus
Surface: 5.5 ha (13.5 acres)

The restored Alumnae Valley reclaims its place in the natural hydrological system that structures the Wellesley College campus. Not merely a restoration, the re-conceptualization of the site includes an understanding of its history, from glacial valley to industrial dumping ground to parking lot. The dual role of topography on the site—both a means to a design solution and an experiential enhancement—forms the foundation of a landscape that is at once willfully artificial and unabashedly picturesque.

When Frederick Law Olmsted Jr. surveyed Wellesley College in 1902, he saw a topography of glacial landforms, valley meadows, and native plant communities—campus characteristics he emphatically suggested be preserved. During the initial years of the college's development, the area now known as Alumnae Valley was a neglected remnant of that original landscape. Neglect soon became indifference, and in the ensuing decades the valley became the site for the college's physical plant, industrialized natural gas pumping, and ultimately, a parking lot over a toxic brownfield.

The Alumnae Valley landscape represents seven years of work on the 5.5-hectares area of the campus. The restoration confronts a history of contamination on this site and results in a new, ecologically functioning landscape structured by a remedial purification system. In 1997 a Master Plan was prepared for the college. In that report, the valley—at that time a parking lot for 175 cars—was marked as a potential area for new campus development. The siting of a campus center building to the north and a newfound focus on the pedestrian experience heightened the importance of the valley as both a visual and physical link among the hilltop nodes of campus life.

The construction of a parking garage in association with the new campus center relieved the site of its burden as a car corral. However, the site's toxic history was embedded in its soil. Removal of the asphalt parking lot promised to exhume the contaminants, as did excavation for the new structures. Hazardous soil was dealt with in two ways in the project design: removal and in situ treatment. Heavily toxic soil was located, excavated, and removed offsite for treatment. Dense non-aqueous phase liquid, a byproduct of natural gas processing, had found

the ancient watershed beneath the parking lot and collected there. Pumping infrastructure was incorporated into the design, and toxic residue is periodically removed for treatment. Capped with clean fill, mildly contaminated soils could be kept on site and used as fill for a trio of meadow-planted, drumlin-like mounds. As a result, the entire site was raised 1.8 meters above the previous grade and a new wetland, the engine of our design, was artificially perched. Toxicity caused many problems, and each inspired a creative solution.

Parallel to the passive neglect of the 20th century ran the destruction of the site's original hydrology that Olmsted so admired. The valley's role as a link between its 32-hectare watershed and the adjacent Lake Waban was broken by an access road. The valley, after the project, is once again an intermittent wetland and more; a series of sedimentation forebays and basins hold and treat the site runoff water, which mingles with forbs, sedges, and cattails before trickling back into Lake Waban. A geosynthetic clay liner simultaneously seals contaminated soils and prevents water from prematurely returning to the original water table.

Munger Valley

Davis Museum

Physical Plant

Severance Green

3

12

Toxic Soil Removed

Toxic Soil Capped

Toxic Soil Removed

Tower Court

9

10

11

Toxic Soil Removed

Lake House

6

Boat House

ake Waban

LÍTHICA – Reclamation of the s'Hostal Quarries

Location:
Pedreres de s'Hostal,
Ciutadella de Menorca,
Balearic Islands, Spain
Plan: 1996–99
Implementation:
2000–03, 2004–07,
2008–11
Ordering party:
Asociación Líthica
Project team:
Laetitia Lara (architect
and sculptor, in charge
of the overall project);
Austín Petschen (architect,
jointly responsible for
the architectural projects
in the years 1997–2009;
architect of the information
pavilion); Virginia Pallarés
(architect, since 2009
Laetitia Lara's collaborator
for architectural projects);
José Bravo (landscape
architect in charge of the
Laberint dels Vergers,
the umbrella project that
includes all the work
for the regeneration
of green areas and creation
of gardens)
Collaborators:
Ayuntamiento
de Ciutadella, Consell
Insular de Menorca, Govern
de les Illes Balears,
Leader-Illa de Menorca,
Obra Social Sa Nosta-Caixa
de Balears
Previous use: Quarry
Current use:
Public park, cultural center,
regenerated green areas
Surface: 5.5 ha (13.5 acres)

The Island of Minorca, the northernmost isle in the Balearic archipelago, is a world
to itself in which nature and man have jointly shaped the landscape over
the centuries, leaving their mark on stone. Marvels of nature—cliffs, grottoes,
and the ubiquitous rocks—stand side by side with man-made ones: caves carved
into the rock, *taula, talayot*, dry stonewalls running for kilometers on end and
ashlar buildings made from *piedra de marés*, the sandstone typical of the area.
Set within this rocky landscape are the sandstone quarries: spaces dug into the
ground in which century after century, block after block, the local stoneworkers
carved out the material required for building work on the island. Some of these
are underground quarries (for hand-extraction), while others are open-air ones
(for hand-extraction or mechanical extraction).
The s'Hostal quarries are located a short distance away from Ciutadella de Menorca.
The 5.5-hectare area is dotted with open-air sandstone quarries—some for
hand-extraction, others for manual extraction. An upper level encircles the deep pits.
After two hundred years, the extraction work ceased in 1994, leaving
an abandoned landscape carved in stone at s'Hostal, which was threatened
with a future of rubble and rubbish.

Líthica
In November 2004 the architect and sculptor Laetitia Sauleau Lara, together
with various people from the world of art and architecture, founded
the association Líthica, which started renting the s'Hostal quarries with the aim
of protecting, regenerating and enhancing them, in such a way as to promote
the sandstone quarries of Minorca.
Líthica's work rests on an acknowledgement of the outstanding artistic value
of the quarries as a landscape cut into stone, a testimony to the extraction work
performed, and a genuine example of rock architecture—a large labyrinth dug
into the ground, a green area both wild and cultivated.
After a few years of struggle to obtain the withdrawal of the restoration project
required by the current legislation (and calling for the complete filling up
of the quarries), in an attempt to raise public awareness of the issue
and promote the site, it was finally possible to begin the regeneration work
on the s'Hostal quarries.
The project aims to reinforce the essence of the quarry as a stone landscape by
recovering and reinterpreting its legacy of quarrying and rock architecture. In other
words, the project aims to open the area up through the extraction of stone.
In line with this philosophy, the stage of the amphitheater was enlarged by
extracting more stone—which was then used for new buildings—in order to lower
the level of the surrounding surface. The safety walls surrounding the modern
quarries are made from sandstone blocks arranged in such a way as to recreate
the typical outline of quarry walls. The access ramp to the modern area is furnished
with a safety wall created by lowering the surface level. The reception pavilion
is a sandstone structure. The infrastructures inside the modern quarries that will be
housing spectacles and workshops have been designed as spaces dug out
of the rock. Signs cut in stone help visitors find their way within the new space.
The maze of excavated spaces characterizing the old area is covered in a lush
vegetation, shielded from the strong winds. This sector has been the focus
of the Laberinto de los Vergeles project, which entailed the regeneration

of the green areas and the creation of gardens by respecting and strengthening the existing natural environment, while at the same time reviving the Minorcan tradition of planting vegetables in the quarries. Furthermore, gardens have been set up as cultural and educational areas for the protection of the native flora of the Island of Minorca, as in the case of the Botanical Circuit and Medieval Garden.

Visitors to the s'Hostal quarries enter a real labyrinth. All of Líthica's work in the area respects or indeed reinforces the maze-like quality of the quarries. The main aim of Líthica's project is to preserve the quarries from demolition by lending them new life as a living heritage, a place to be visited and made use of every day of the year, and a setting and framework for cultural events—be they music concerts, theater plays, ballets or sculpture exhibits. This is conceived as a place in which to organize meetings, youth events and sport activities in which everyone can take part.

Urban Outfitters Headquarters

Location:
Philadelphia Navy Yard,
Pennsylvania
Plan: 2004
Implementation: 2005–11
Ordering party:
Urban Outfitters Inc.
Project team: D.I.R.T.
studio: Julie Bargmann
(principal-in-charge);
David Hill (project
landscape architect)
Collaborators:
Engineering: Advanced
GeoServices; *landscape
contractor:* Turning Leaf;
Meyer Scherer
& Rockcastle (MS&R
architect)
Previous use: Shipyard
Current use:
Campus, design studios,
public park
Surface: 3.8 ha (9.4 acres)

Historic core

The Urban Outfitters headquarters reclaims 3.8 hectares of land within
the 162-hectare decommissioned US Navy Shipyard at League Island
in Philadelphia. D.I.R.T. studio collaborated with a team of architects, engineers
and contractors from early conceptual design through construction administration
to establish the new corporate campus centered around five renovated buildings
and a 146-meter-long dry-dock where Philadelphia's central axis of Broad Street
meets the Delaware River.

This productive landscape holds the central territory of League Island, between
a still-active shipyard and mixed-use redevelopment. While the Navy sailed away
from the island in 1996, they left the industrial bones of the site intact. Partially
buried in a sea of asphalt over one mile of old rail lines and crane-ways provide
an arabesque counter to 152-meter-long monolithic brick buildings. This rich
material palette and the landscape structure were essential for unifying the extent
of the Urban Outfitters (URBN) campus, and rooting it in the scale and history
of the Yard.

The URBN campus plants a seed of creative vitality in the heart of the Navy Yard.
The landscape structure of five long north-south hedgerows and amplified street
edges along with a finer cross-grain of gardens and terraces unifies the campus,
engaging the scale of the Navy Yard while simultaneously supporting an intimacy
of daily occupation. A central lawn doubling as a dog park offers employees
and visitors space for informal meeting, recreation and relaxation. These spaces
build on URBN's desire to cultivate a strong creative culture for its over 600
employees.

At the overlap between the campus and the river, the phased development
of the central dry dock expands the city's connection to the waterfront through
a new public garden and terrace. This increased accessibility and creative
presence on the former industrial site make URBN a poster child
for the Philadelphia Industrial Development Corporation's (PIDC) efforts
to transform the 486-hectare industrial property. The campus is already public
attraction, challenging visitors' expectations of the Navy Yard's future role
in the city and the regenerative potential for other industrialized landscapes across
the country.

When it came to selecting materials for the URBN headquarters, site forensics
unearthed a "life cycle" palette: appliquéd asphalt, age-old concrete, tired brick,
rusted metal grates, peeling surfaces of text and enough residue to reconstruct
this industrial-strength landscape. Rather than "hog and haul"—or excavation
and disposal—of a typical demolition plan, a salvaging strategy was deployed,
harvesting what most would consider undesirable detritus. No imported materials
were necessary, or desired. Full-scale mock-ups challenged construction-as-usual
techniques and became critical in developing strategies for reuse that were both
compelling and cost effective. The crushed leftovers of smaller bits of concrete,
asphalt and brick became calico-colored mulch at the base of the very long
hedgerows of native trees.

1. COUNT:
embodied energy

2. UNEARTH:
directed salvage

3. PILE:
760 cubic yards

4. RE-PLACE:
reconfigured ground

5. BRAND:
barney rubble

6. SEEP:
780% more porous

Embodied energy
The URBN campus expands the client's aesthetic pursuit of material reinvention
to establish a broader capacity for ecological performance. The Yard's expanse
of concrete and asphalt was refashioned onsite, saving 581 cubic meters of waste
from landfills and increasing site perviousness from 55 to more than 4000 square
meters. This new urban sponge structures a network of bioswales running
from the campus to the river and supports hedgerows that shade western
building facades. The multi-functioning site infrastructure continues
the productivity of the ground, preserving and reinterpreting the energy
embodied by thousands of workers past and present.

Olympic Sculpture Park

Location: Seattle, Washington
Plan: 2001
Implementation: 2007
Ordering party:
Seattle Art Museum
Project team:
Site design/architecture:
Weiss/Manfredi;
*Architecture/Landscape/
Urbanism:* Marion Weiss
and Michael A. Manfredi
(design partners),
Christopher Ballentine
(project manager),
Todd Hoehn and Yehre Suh
(project architects),
Patrick Armacost, Michael
Blasberg, Emily Clanahan,
Lauren Crahan, Beatrice
Eleazar, Kian Goh, Hamilton
Hadden, Mike Harshman,
Mustapha Jundi, Justin
Kwok, John Peek,
and Akari Takebayashi
Collaborators:
*Structural and civil
engineering:* Magnusson
Klemencic Associates;
*mechanical and electrical
engineering:* ABACUS
Engineered Systems;
lighting design: Brandston
Partnership Inc.; *general
contractor:* Sellen
Construction, Seattle, WA;
*geotechnical engineering
consultancy:* Hart Crowser,
Seattle, WA; *environment
consultancy:* Aspect
Consulting, Seattle, WA;
aquatic engineering

Envisioned as a new urban model for sculpture parks, this project is located on Seattle's last undeveloped waterfront property—an industrial brownfield site sliced by train tracks and an arterial road. The design connects three separate sites with an uninterrupted Z-shaped "green" platform, descending 12 meters from the city to the water, capitalizing on views of the skyline and Elliott Bay, and rising over existing infrastructure to reconnect the urban core to the revitalized waterfront.

Formerly owned by Union Oil of California (Unocal), the area was used as an oil transfer facility. Before construction of the park, over 120,000 tons of contaminated soil were removed. The remaining petroleum contaminated soil is capped by a new landform with over 153,000 cubic meters of clean fill, much of it excavated from the Seattle Art Museum's downtown expansion project. Winner of an international design competition, the design for the Olympic Sculpture Park capitalizes on the 12-meter grade change from the top of the site to the water's edge. Planned as a continuous landscape that wanders from the city to the shoreline, this Z-shaped hybrid landform provides a new pedestrian infrastructure. Built with a system of mechanically stabilized earth, the enhanced landform re-establishes the original topography of the site, as it crosses the highway and train tracks and descends to meet the city. Layered over the existing site and infrastructure, the scheme creates a dynamic link that makes the waterfront accessible. The main pedestrian route is initiated at a 1670-square-meter exhibition pavilion and descends as each leg of the path opens to radically different views. The first stretch crosses a highway, offering views of the Olympic Mountains; the second crosses the train tracks, offering views of the city and port; and the last descends to the water, opening views of the newly created beach. This pedestrian landform now allows free movement between the city's urban center and the restored beaches at the waterfront.

As the route descends from the pavilion to the water, it links three distinct settings: a dense and temperate evergreen forest; a deciduous forest of seasonally changing characteristics; and a shoreline garden including a series of new tidal terraces for salmon habitat and saltwater vegetation. Throughout the park, landforms and plantings collaborate to direct, collect, and cleanse storm water as it moves through the site before being discharged into Elliott Bay.

As a "landscape for art," the Olympic Sculpture Park defines a new experience for modern and contemporary art outside the museum walls. The topographically varied park provides diverse settings for sculpture of multiple scales. Deliberately open-ended, the design invites new interpretations of art and environmental engagement, reconnecting the fractured relationships of art, landscape, and urban life.

consultancy: Anchor Environmental, Seattle, WA; *graphics consultancy:* Pentagram, New York, NY; *security and AV/IT consultancy:* ARUP, New York, NY; *catering & food service consultancy:* Bon Appetit, Seattle, WA; *kitchen consultancy:* JLR Design, Seattle, WA; *retail consultancy:* Doyle + Associates, Philadelphia, PA; *project management:* Barrientos LLC, Seattle, WA; *architectural site representation:* Owens Richards Architects, pllc, Seattle, WA
Previous use:
Industrial site
Current use:
Public park: olympic sculpture park
Surface: 3.64 ha (9 acres)
Cost: 17 million dollars

Gargas Ochre Mines

Location:
Bruoux, Gargas, France
Plan: 2005
Implementation: 2009
Ordering party:
Municipality of Gargas
Project team:
Landscape design:
Christine Dalnoky; *interior
design:* DeSo – Defrain
Souquet; *structural
engineering:* Nathalie
Capelli
Previous use: Ochre mine
Current use: Touristic site
Surface: 3.5 ha (8.6 acres)
Cost: 1.5 million euros

The city of Gargas is located in Southern France and is home to the site
of Bruoux, where the architecture firm DeSo and Christine Dalnoky's architectural
and landscaping project was built.
The site is predominantly made up of a natural mineral: ochre, pure clay combined
with ferric rock and used as a coloring pigment since prehistory.
The rock makes this region a unique "Provençal Colorado" recognized
as a biosphere reserve by UNESCO.
It is an unusual location—as well as the esthetic power generated by the work
of 19th-century miners.
Today, Gargas is still one of the last few villages in Europe where ochre is still
exploited. The transformation of Bruoux's mines into an organized tour is designed
in an effort to enhance a mining heritage bound up with the present.
The development was designed in such a way that the visitor's eye can capture
a whole range of elements, colors and materials, an immersion intended
by the designers.
To achieve that effect, the designers constructed the reception building by shifting
it leftward, so as to avoid screening the view of the cliff.
A power substation in the immediate field of vision, at man-size level,
at the entrance of the site, was concealed by a brown wire mesh in order to blend
in with the surrounding natural range of colors. The substation was shut in
with ochre concrete low walls from the site, thus avoiding import—a highly
environment-friendly commitment.
Miners carved away at the outside walls of the cliffs and were thus able to clear
platforms outside the gallery entrances.
It is a large slope that sweeps down to the foot of the cliff.
The architect and landscapist capitalized on these carvings by building
an "amphitheater promenade" including stair-like layered tiers to accommodate
art festivals.
Like the outside developments, the inside developments of the mines were also
simple, pared-down and free of any pervasive detail effects.
An ochre light-colored concrete retaining wall built on the hillside makes up
an "amenity-based" layer comprising the exterior patios.
The building has a vegetated roof to:
- achieve a harmonious match and integration of the construction in the natural
environment;
- obtain superior thermal inertia of the overall system;
- ventilate the building simply and manually;
- use waste water from the vegetated roof and return the runoffs to the site.

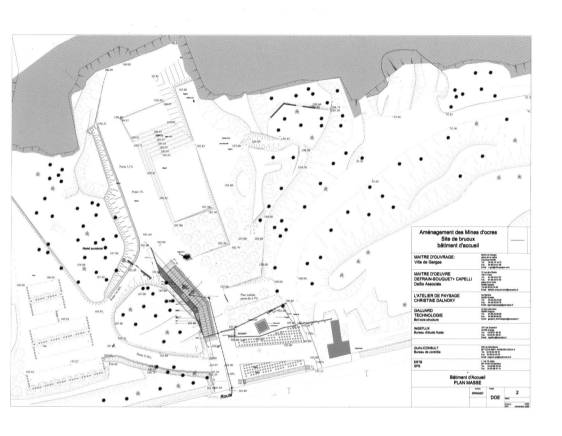

Whitney Water Purification Facility and Park

Location: New Haven, CT
Plan: 1998
Implementation:
1998–2005
Ordering party: South
Central Connecticut
Regional Water Authority,
New Haven, CT
Project team:
Michael Van Valkenburgh
Associates (MVVA):
Matthew Urbanski (design
principal); Michael Van
Valkenburgh (managing
principal); A. Paul Seck
(senior associate);
Robert Rock (associate);
J.P. Weesner. Architecture:
Steven Holl Architects
New York, NY; civil
engineering: Tighe and
Bond Consulting Engineers
Westfield, MA; structural
engineering: CH2M Hill
Boston, MA;
construction manager:
C.H. Nickerson &
Company, Inc.
Torrington, CT; landscape
contractor: Emanouil
Brothers, Inc.
Chelmsford, MA;
bioengineering consultancy:
The Bioengineering Group,
Inc. Salem, MA
Previous use:
Water treatment facility
Current use:
Water treatment facility
and public park
Surface: 5.7 ha (14 acres)
Cost: 2.9 million dollars

Located on the suburban outskirts of New Haven, the facility is a reserve water source for the South Central Connecticut Regional Water Authority. It draws water from nearby Lake Whitney, at the base of the Mill River Watershed. The site is adjacent to the Eli Whitney Museum, which commemorates the famous inventor and his son, who first dammed the adjacent Mill River for use as a water supply in 1806.

The use of the most elemental of landscape architectural tools—soil, water, and plants—offsets the sleek form of the facility building. The design creates topographical variety and interest through sustainable reuse of excavated soil. Swales replace a traditional engineered drainage system. The planting program, inspired by restoration ecology, is at once primal and sophisticated in its extent and complexity.

The new topography is stabilized using bio-engineering methods. Site stormwater and runoff from the building's green roof are filtered as they move through the landscape. The planting scheme uses native species that require no fertilizers or pesticides, reducing the facility's impact downstream. The plant palette is also calibrated for seasonal variation in color and texture, and anticipates the natural evolution of plant communities over time.

The landscape is designed to be a didactic microcosm of the entire regional watershed. The swales guide site runoff through a series of discrete landscapes—including farmland, meadow, and valley stream—before collecting it in a new pond that recharges the groundwater table. Meandering footpaths allow visitors to move through this narrative and consider how water interacts with the land. While the utility is privately owned, the landscape architecture and building work to engage, rather than ignore, the adjacent residential neighborhood. The site also hosts the historic Eli Whitney Barn, a space for community events and programming. By transforming a formerly flat lawn into a dynamic, ecologically diverse public space, the design improves longstanding community use of the grounds, and integrates the site with its suburban surroundings.

Collaborative landscape
strategy places 70% of
building below grade

40,000 cubic yards of displaced
soil from building excavation
creates new topography

Topography harnesses natural
hydrological processes to
improve water quality

A diverse landscape
becomes a neighborhood
amenity

1   Pre-existing Wetlands
2   Lake
3   Island
4   Peninsula
5   Beach
6   Gorge
7   Valley & Stream
8   Agricultural Garden
9   Mountain & Intermittent Stream

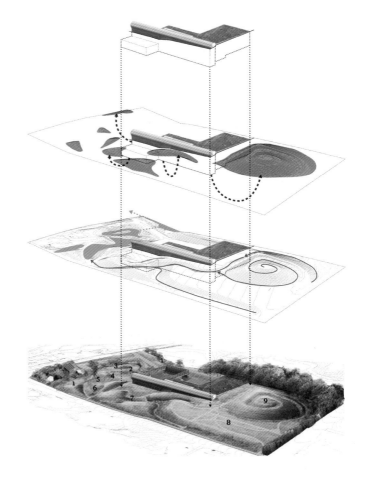

St. Margarethen Quarry

Location:
St. Margarethen, Austria
Plan: 2005 (competition),
start of construction 2006
Implementation: 2008
Ordering party:
Fürst Esterházy
Familienprivatstiftung
Project team: AllesWirdGut
Architektur ZT GmbH
Collaborators:
Architectural engineering:
Ecki Csallner, Elmir Smajic,
Ferdinand Kersten, Maria
Magina, Mareike
Kuchenbecker, Martin
Brandt, Michael Sohm;
structural engineering:
Gmeiner Haferl ZT GmbH;
building services:
HPD Planungsdienst;
infrastructure:
Bichler&Kolbe ZT GmbH;
project management: FCP
Fritsch Chiari ZT GmbH
Consultants:
structural physics:
DI Prause; *geotechnical
engineering:* 3P
Geotechnik; *lighting design:*
Klaus Pokorny; *kitchen
design:* Büro Stria; *escape
route planning:* Büro Düh
Previous use: Quarry
Current use:
Auditorium for outdoor
concerts
Surface:
0.56 ha gross floor area -
0.44 ha outdoor spaces
(1.4 acres)

It is difficult to realize that this impressive scenery—which is characterized by precise cutting-edge, exactly worked surfaces and well-advised subtraction of the ground—is only a by-product of old-age mining resources.
The rock itself is used as building material, as much as possible. From the first contact of the visitor in the notch of the parking, the stone becomes a wall. Quarry-related materials and materials from the quarry itself are used predominantly for the surfaces of the free spaces. In the foyer visitors find a carpet made of different sorts of grit, which are converted into a water bound cover. This guarantees the necessary infiltration areas and avoids formation of dust during the dry summer months.
All the added cubatures and edges are covered with oxidized steel-plates, a material which is historically used in the quarry. Associations with heavy construction machinery come naturally to mind.
By virtue of the different regional origins of the specific parts of the structure, various construction methods have been used.
The backstage area, with its complicated access and the limited elbowroom, is a timber-wood construction. It has been possible to deliver prefab elements, inclusive of all the necessary facade plates, into the construction site.
Those could then be brought in to the construction site over the cliffs via a crane. The allocation of the backstage area into two separate parts allows two different construction phases, according to requirements.

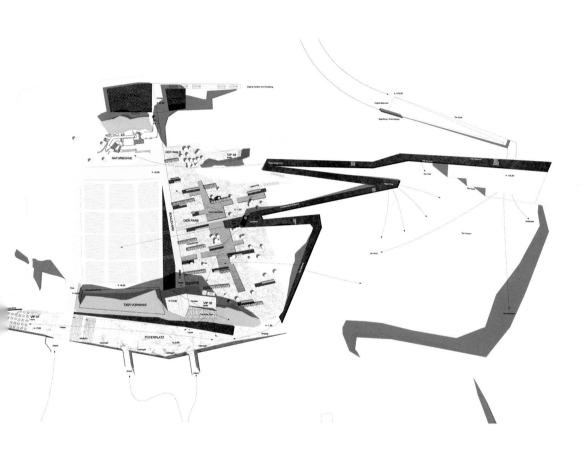

1 ha

The Recycled Landscape as Prosthetic Landscape

Guido Incerti

Prosthesis: A prosthesis is an artificial device that replaces a missing body part. (*Wikipedia*)

The human being is a *prosthetic* being that each day absorbs new elements, both material and immaterial, to nourish his life experience. The knowledge of this experience is always embodied: it is experienced and transformed into an essence that may be described as concrete and which emerges through the action of a body across space and time. This action related to experience engenders constant transformations not just in man's psyche and knowledge, but also on the bodily level through a physicality which—in many human experiences—feels the need to enclose body parts within the landscape as much as the landscape in the body, as Durkheim[1] noted in relation to tattoos and elementary forms of religion.

The human body is a landscape which, just like the anthropic landscape, can be constantly transformed, influenced, improved or even damaged through this prosthetic system deriving from psychological and physical experiences: through his own body man experiences the same condition that the landscape which he inhabits experiences; he is driven by desire, by the prospect of well-being, yet at the same time he is more or less aware of the damage inflicted upon his body, and the surrounding world, by his achievements.

This is the tragedy of contemporary life, and perhaps one of the dilemmas of modernity. A constant tension between attraction and repulsion, enticement and fear that is perfectly encapsulated by the *prosthetic condition* we find ourselves in.

By the expression *prosthetic condition* of the landscape I wish to refer to the kind of expedients that, starting from the urban environment—the human prosthesis par excellence, justified by the need for subsistence at first and then by economic factors—have led to man's *shaping of the landscape* and to the perceptual process related to this through the "bodily projection" of the self upon the surrounding space.

While all cognitive processes conceive of the body as the fundamental three-dimensional *gizmo* through which the human being can move on the earthly plane, the body is also the chief tool for the transformation of the landscape according to man's will. When engaging with the planning—or rather regeneration—of a landscape damaged by the above-described modern condition, why not draw a parallel, then, between the prosthesis/body symbiosis and the prosthesis/landscape one?

The recycling of the landscape, which is now acknowledged as a requirement for zero-volume policies, and the re-use of abandoned, contaminated or rubbish-filled areas show that the landscape can be envisaged as dross to be salvaged, as a residue of the post-modern condition. As such, it can be put back on the market. It must be recycled and improved. It must be transformed in such a way as to serve different functions, which paradoxically coincide with those which modernity—now globalization—has made available by freeing man from the slavery of work.

Many of the projects collected in the *Atlas* concern areas that are unproductive in terms of the economic manufacture of consumer or agricultural goods, but productive when it comes to the possibility of satisfying human beings and their leisure time, even more so than the sheer need for natural spaces.

And herein lies yet another feature of the recycled landscape as *prosthetic landscape*.

Recycled landscapes are in all respects the product of landscapes damaged by human activities—usually consciously so—with regard to which human beings first started feeling a sense "of unease"[2] and then, following the "green" revolution stemming from man's conquest of space,[3] a desire for reconquest deriving from a newly acquired awareness of the finiteness of the Earth in relation to space.

This unease and awareness with regard to the uniqueness of the system Earth—which are hardly perceived any longer, judging at any rate from the guidelines laid down by the Italian Ministry of the Environment in the recent document *Elementi per una Strategia Nazionale di Adattamento ai Cambiamenti Climatici* (Towards a National Strategy of Adaptation to Climate Change)[4]—have fostered the need to regenerate and newly transform the landscape in the pursuit of the virginity which it and we ourselves have lost.

To extend this parallel with the human body, we might describe this regeneration and recycling as an operation of "landscape hymenoplasty" whereby a planner seeks to regenerate, embellish and improve parts of the landscape as though he/she were rebuilding, improving and embellishing her (or his) beloved to bring her/him back to the state prior to the defloration carried out, upon the body of the landscape, by modern and global society and economy.[5]

This process of recycling and transformation may also be envisaged as a "surgery," because in contemporary society projects seldom follow the development of nature and the environment over time, since they constitute operations that are meant to treat a human sense of unease, and ways of turning the landscape and environment into an active, driving background to urban planning. As such, in order to be implemented, these operations require a different time frame, a period of human recovery which will enable a *discharge* "here and now"—as opposed to the slow time frame of natural evolution.

The recycled landscape, therefore, is not only a prosthetic landscape because it is mended and reconstructed, but also because it in turn serves as an agent for urban and territorial regeneration in post-industrial cities, life sap for damaged tissues.

In most cases these deteriorated, fragmented connective tissues are marked—just like the human body—by forms of degeneration such as abandonment, over-exploitation, pollution. These pathologies have affected the very nature of the landscape and of cities, in some cases altering their DNA completely. One striking example is the Brick Pit Ring. Here, an industrial site near Sydney has experienced a prosthetic surgical recovery process: this was achieved with the closure of industrial plants, on the one side, and re-naturalization and re-use through a series of light structures in a project by Durback Block, on the other.

Recycling, then, may be viewed as a treatment for the physical degeneration of an area which is not given the time to regenerate itself. Recycling is a contemporary treatment for both the human body and the landscape.

The human body and the landscape cannot be experienced as separate elements: for it is man's perception in moving across space, man's interpretation of its structure, that engenders the "landscape"—just as the human body is the result of the development of the landscape. This concept is clearly expressed in Chinese calligraphy, where the ideogram for "man"—*ren*, written like the Japanese *hito*, which also has the same meaning—derives from the stylization of the human body depicted in terms of the one feature that makes it unique: as an erect walking figure. And if we turn to consider the original character, what we find is the profile of a human being.[6] According to certain palaeoanthropological theories,[7] this posture developed thanks to the marked morphological plasticity of the human skeleton, which ensured its adaptation to climate changes and the consequent environmental transformations which hominids experienced during their evolution. The ancestors of *Homo sapiens* were forced to stand on their two hind legs when in east Africa—over the course of several thousand years—they were forced to descend from trees to adapt to the new environment that was taking shape: the savannah. This morphological change was necessary in order to acquire a new perspective: to gaze beyond the tall grass and shrubs marking the new landscape, to spot carcasses yet unspoilt by predators—since meat had become part of the human diet, but man was not yet a hunter. Our ancestors had no need for this behavior when they were still living on trees in equatorial forests.

According to some evolutionary theories, the defining physical feature of the human body and its perceptual capacity is ultimately a consequence of the transformation of the landscape.

The landscape thus triggered the evolutionary transition which eventually led man to explore and dominate the world—and to plan the landscape, as we experience it today.

A natural transformation, then, led to a morphological and anatomical mutation, which enabled our ancestors to walk with an erect posture, and hence to more easily travel, measure, quantify, plan and alter the world. Within this world, the landscape has always been recycled, transformed, and developed: it has always been *prosthetic*.

The regeneration and transformation of the body we are now experiencing, just like the regeneration and recycling of the landscape, are two

facets of the same process of projection, which acquires a prosthetic quality in relation to the human body, and vice-versa. Human bodies nowadays require operations of regeneration and self-regeneration through aesthetic surgery—in some cases extremely invasive operations, in others only a light touching-up—that will allow planners— following Rogozov's example[8]—to insert some prostheses that may sooth the pain we have inflicted upon our body and help us turn present bodies and landscapes into future post-bodies and post-landscapes.

[1] E. Durkheim, *Le forme elementari della vita religiosa*, Biblioteca Meltemi, Meltemi Editore, Rome 2005.

[2] Freud explored this notion in psychoanalytical terms in *Civilization and Its Discontents*, 1930.

[3] M. McLuhan and Q. Fiore, *Guerra e pace nel villaggio globale*, Apogeo, Milan 1995.

[4] http://www.minambiente.it

[5] One is reminded here of *Death Becomes Her*, the film Robert Zemeckis directed in 1992, in which the female protagonist takes revenge on her longtime rival thanks to her knowledge of the elixir of life—a knowledge that inevitably brings about the ruin of almost all the characters in the story.

[6] M. Bussagli, *L'uomo nello spazio*, Medusa Edizioni, Milan 2005.

[7] F. Facchini, *Antropologia*, Utet, Turin 1988, 1995.

[8] Quoted by G.Teyssot, *The Mutant body of Architecture*, in E. Diller and S. Scofidio, *Flesh, Architectural Probes*, Princeton Architectural Press, New York 1994. A member of the sixth Soviet Antarctic expedition in 1961, Leonid Rogozov self-diagnosed an appendicitis. Being the only qualified doctor in that remote region, he removed his own appendix by making a 12-cm incision on his abdomen. The surgery was conducted with the help of an assistant (a specialized mechanic), who throughout the operation held a mirror at a 45-degree angle, to enable Rogozov to see his own inner organs. Rogozov's approach to his body during the operation was marked by a peculiar distance, achieved through the use of a local anesthetic, which enabled him to define a new relation between body, patient, and surgeon.

Braga Stadium

Location:
Monte Crasto, Parque Norte, Braga, Portugal
Plan: 2000
Implementation: 2002–03
Ordering party:
Câmara Municipal de Braga
Project team:
Architecture: Souto Moura – Arquitectos, Lda; Eduardo Souto de Moura; Carlo Nozza; Ricardo Merí, Enrique Penichet, Atsushi Hoshima, Diego Setien, Carmo Correia, Sérgio Koch, Joaquim Portela, Luisa Rosas, Jorge Domingues, Adriano Pimenta, Ricardo Rosa Santos, Diogo Guimarães, José Carlos Mariano, João Queiroz e Lima, Tiago Coelho; *landscaping:* Daniel Monteiro; *engineering:* Afassociados – Projectos de Engenharia, SA
Collaborators:
Stadium Program: Arup Associates – Dipesh Patel
Previous use: Quarrry
Current use: Stadium
Surface: 0.7 ha (1.8 acres); 30,000 seats
Cost: 75 million euros

The Braga Municipal Stadium is situated within the Dume Sports Park on the northern slope of Monte Castro.
The location was chosen in order to avoid making a dam along the water's edge in the valley. The alternative would have been to move it further to the west up against the hill, like a Roman amphitheater.
Nowadays football is a big entertainment, hence the decision to have only two rows of seats.
Initially the roof was to look like a long continuous visor (ref. Siza / Expo), but it was eventually modeled on the Peruvian Inca bridges.
With a height of 40 meters, the stadium is built against two squares with the same sloping. This enables the stadium building to serve as an anchor point for any future development in the area, as the city expands northwards.

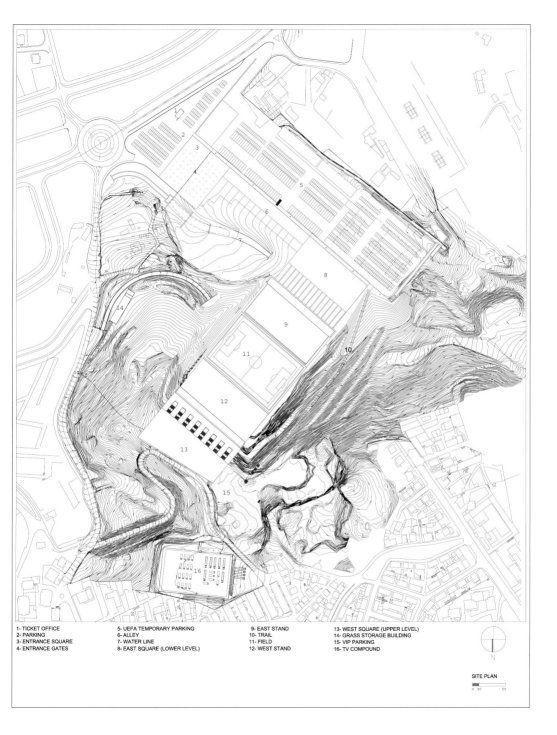

1- TICKET OFFICE
2- PARKING
3- ENTRANCE SQUARE
4- ENTRANCE GATES

5- UEFA TEMPORARY PARKING
6- ALLEY
7- WATER LINE
8- EAST SQUARE (LOWER LEVEL)

9- EAST STAND
10- TRAIL
11- FIELD
12- WEST STAND

13- WEST SQUARE (UPPER LEVEL)
14- GRASS STORAGE BUILDING
15- VIP PARKING
16- TV COMPOUND

SITE PLAN

0 10   50

N

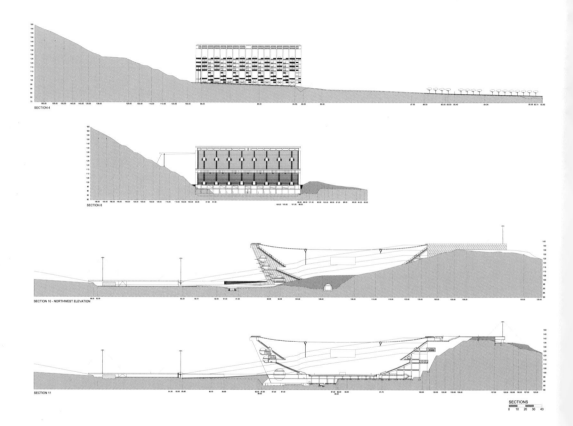

SECTION 4

SECTION 6

SECTION 10 - NORTHWEST ELEVATION

SECTION 11

SECTIONS
0   10   20   30   40

Le Gallerie di Piedicastello / The Trento Tunnels

Location: Trento, Italy
Plan: 2007–09
Implementation: 2009
Ordering party:
Fondazione Museo Storico
del Trentino, Trento:
Giuseppe Ferrandi (director),
Patrizia Marchesoni
(curator for Provincia
Autonoma di Trento)
Project team:
*Interdisciplinary
Transatlantic Tunnel project
team*: Terragni Architetti,
Jeffrey T. Schnapp Stanford
Humanities Lab, FilmWork,
Gruppe Gut

An experiment in the redevelopment of an industrial site, a reinvention of the history museum, an animated archive, an act of healing of a tear in the urban fabric, teaching gardens born in an asphalt crib: the Trento Tunnels project (Le Gallerie) is all this and more.

This project reinterprets a fragment of transportation infrastructure, converting it from vehicular to pedestrian use. It accompanies this shift with a program of city gardens that serve as boundary markers. The southern garden features the flora of the Veronese border to the south. The northern one, situated along the edge of the new highway access to the city, takes on the form of an Alpine garden. The gardens' role is thus not only to instruct about the Trentino region's flora, but to transfigure the tunnels into symbols of a region that serves as a conduit between the Mediterranean South and the Germanic North. They do so in a manner that excavates even deeper stratified meanings that transcend the site: the cognitive, emotive, and symbolic resonances of tunnels and tunneling. Thanks to the minimalism of the interventions carried out, two 300-meter-long galleries become "galleries" in the sense of palaces of memory and places

Collaborators:
Terragni Architetti:
Elisabetta Terragni, Paola
Frigerio, Simone Zbudil
Bonatti, Bret Walliser,
Diego Magri; Stanford
Humanities Lab: Jeffrey
T. Schnapp, Jeffrey Aldrich
(design and second life
production); FilmWork:
Luca dal Bosco, Carlo dal
Bosco, Lorenzo Pevarello,
Giovanni Agostini, Linnea
Merzagora, Pierpaolo
Ferlaino, Mariano de Tassis
(lighting designer);
Gruppe Gut: Alfonso
Demetz, Uli Prugger,
Werner Stampfer, Katrin
Gruber
Previous use:
Transport infrastructure
Current use:
History exhibitions space,
theme park
Surface: 0.65 ha (1.6 acres)
Cost: 1.3 million euros

of aesthetic play. To enter them is to travel back in time through the 20th century and its material remains. To see the light at their end is to espy the seam where a territory's history meets its present. And this mining of the tunnels' expressive force meshes with the development of a flexible interior architecture that complements innovative museological strategies that have transformed Le Gallerie into a history laboratory. This 7000-square-meter laboratory arises at a location that is doubly marked: marked with respect to the city's entryway, located as it is under the Doss Trento with its monuments and mausoleums; marked also with respect to the city's social history inasmuch as the tunnels' construction in the 1970s split one of Trento's historical neighborhoods in two. The project merges restoration with renewal.

The first edition
Inaugurated in August 2008, Le Gallerie were launched with a show on the memory of the First World War entitled *I Trentini e la Grande Guerra*, narrated from the standpoint of ordinary individuals. To traverse the tunnels was to set out on a march among the dead, documents brought back to life, and objects that survived the decades that separate the present from the war's end. The march took place through parallel tunnels now experienced by pedestrians as they were formerly by automobiles.
The black tunnel contained a phantasmagoria divided into chapters according to the years of the Great War. It wove the voices and images of ordinary people together into a choral account of the war's unfolding. The white tunnel had three sections. The first contained structures modeled after the temporary shelters found in wartime refugee camps, each documenting a moment in the post-war recollection of the First World War: the building of monuments, the foundation of museums, the creation of rituals of remembrance. The second consisted in pedestals hosting material that showed how the war was lived by common citizens. The third was divided between temporary exhibition spaces and pedagogical support structures.

The second edition
Entitled *Storicamente ABC*, the 2009–10 edition was built on the same bifurcation between an immersive black and a didactic white tunnel but with the two decoupled. The exhibition itinerary is now contained within the black tunnel, where a panoramic history of the territory is sectioned into an alphabet, much like a children's book spread out over 300 meters. It is subdivided into a wide passage where sculptural letter/text panel assemblages, supported by video macro- and micro-histories, document themes from A[utonomy] to Z[ambana]; and a narrow passage in which the human topography of the Trentino is "mapped" by a sequence of talking heads. A partition runs the tunnel's length. A new modular system of exhibition spaces and open rooms has been developed for the white tunnel, which now finds its functions multiplied as a meeting hall, performance space, gallery and laboratory.

SNA Saint-Nazaire Alvéole 14

Location:
Alvéole 14, Ville Port
district, Saint-Nazaire,
France
Plan: 1994
Implementation: 2005
Ordering party:
City of Saint-Nazaire
Project team:
Architecture: LIN Finn
Geipel and Giulia Andi
with Hans-Michael Földeak
(project manager)
Collaborators:
Structure: Philippe
Clément, Batiserf,
Grenoble; *building
economy:* Michel Forgue,
Le Rivier d'Apprieu;
fluids: Louis Choulet,
Clemont-Ferrand;
scenography: Gérard
Fleury, Architecture
&Technique, Paris,
Yaying Xu; *acoustics:*
Bruno Suner, Altia
Acoustique, Paris; Robert
Richou, Océanis Ingénierie,
St. Nazaire; *climatic study:*
Matthias Schuler,
Transsolar, Stuttgart;
cultural project: Joseph
Hanimann, Paris
Previous use:
Submarine base
in Saint-Nazaire
Current use:
Venue for contemporary
integrative forms of art
and music
Surface:
0.5 ha (1.2 acres): 0.3 ha
Alvéole 14 + 0.2 ha
public space
Cost:
5.9 million euros
(Alvéole 14), 1.2 million
euros (public space)

The submarine base is located on the estuary of the Loire, near the port of Saint-Nazaire, roughly one kilometer away from the city center. Up until the Second World War, this port at the center of the old city constituted a point of departure for transatlantic voyages to South America. Between 1941 and 1943 the Todt Organization set up a base for German submarines.

The huge bunker—295 meters in length, 130 meters in width and between 15 and 19 meters in height—covers a surface of 3.7 hectares. It is subdivided into 14 sectors (cells): 8 dry docks and 6 floating docks.

The relation between the city and the port was redefined in the 1990s. In 1991 the conceptual artist Yann Kersalé—best known for his work with light—created *La Nuit des Docks*, a lighting project for the industrial harbor.

In 1994 the Ville-Port urban project was launched. Joël Batteux, the Mayor of Saint-Nazaire, centered the future development of the city around the base. During the first stage in the project, Barcelona-based architect Manuel de Solà-Morales opened up the central docks of the base, creating a public boardwalk extending across their surface.

The transformation of the submarine base into a public space – Alvéole 14
The plan calls for the creation of two cultural infrastructures, the LiFE and the VIP, with an inner street running across the base in such a way as to link all its sectors.

The hall of emerging forms (LiFE) is a single, minimalistically equipped space. Since it is located by the old stretch of water, it can be opened up towards the harbor through a large folding gate.

The VIP, a venue for contemporary music, occupies one of the "inner" sections of the base. A hall for 600 people has been designed as a basic cubic space enclosed within a steel frame. This structure houses a reception desk, a bar, some dressing rooms, and an archive.

The inner street running along the route of the old railway line is covered by a "bright carpet." This "gallery," which creates a mysterious atmosphere, links all the key areas of the base, both pre-existing and new ones.

The submarine base is an ambiguous structure: for it acts as both a barrier and a hinge. With its panoramic bridge, the accessible roof of the bunker may serve as a lively space and strategic public area for the city.

From the gallery a stairway leads across the roof to an experimental structure. A geodesic dome from the Berlin Tempelhof Airport is used as a "think tank" for art.

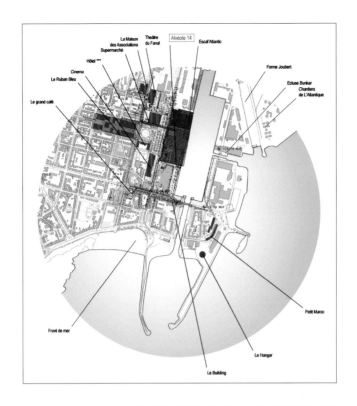

La Maison
des Associations
Supermarché

La Maison
des Associations

Théâtre
du Fanal

Alvéole 14

Escal'Atlantic

Hôtel ***

Cinéma

Le Ruban Bleu

Le grand café

Forme Joubert

Ecluse Bunker

Chantiers
de L'Atlantique

Petit Maroc

Front de mer

Le Hangar

Le Building

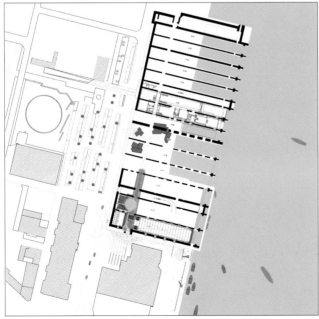

All We Need

Location:
Esch-Belval, Halles des
Soufflantes, Luxembourg
Plan: 2007
Implementation:
21.4.2007–28.10.2007
(exhibition date)
Ordering party:
Luxembourg et Grande
Région, European Capital
of Culture
Project team:
ArGe lux07: Holzer Kobler
Architekturen & iart
interactive
Previous use:
Industrial site
Current use:
Art installation
Surface:
0.5 ha (1.2 acres);
160 m × 70 m × 28 m

All We Need – An exhibition on human needs, resources and fairness
All you need is love… that's not all. *All We Need* explores the world as a global market through the human efforts to dream, imagine and live a happy life. The old Halle des Soufflantes of the Belval Steelworks, an abandoned cathedral of the industrial age, sets the scenery. This exceptional building gave shelter to millions of pigeons and derelict cars before it was transformed into a social and creative space. Within an area of 5000 square meters, the exhibition deals with the questions of human needs, the resources of the planet and a faire globalization. The successful re-invention of this land into a cultural center has resulted in it being highly frequented by a diverse spectrum of visitors.
Without a moral program, the exhibition shows, in particular through the fair trade example, alternatives in consumption and life styles. It provides reflections and proposals for action on the essential questions touching the future of mankind: what are our fundamental needs, and how can we satisfy them without endangering neither the survival of our planet, nor human rights?
Ten large images tell the story of what we daily use and consume:
Relax!, Survive!, Choose!, Protect!, Love!, Belong!, Create!, Understand!, Dream!, Stand Up!

Ravi Marchi Mine in Gavorrano

Location:
Gavorrano, Grosseto, Italy
Plan: 1999
Implementation: 2003
Ordering party:
Regional Government
of Tuscany, Municipality
of Gavorrano
Project team:
Massimo Carmassi with
Gabriella Ioli Carmassi
Collaborators:
Claudio Saragosa,
Salvatore, Christopher
Evans, David Fantini;
mining park project:
Alberto Magnaghi;
structures and plants:
Andrea Gaggiotti and Livio
Gambacorta; *geology:*
Carlo Alberto Garzonio
Previous use: Pyrite mine
Current use: Museum
Surface: 0.4 ha (0.2 acres)

The Ravi Marchi mine and attached buildings for the extraction and processing of pyrite—used for the production of sulphuric acid—are part of the large nature and mining park of Gavorrano on the slope of the metalliferous hills in the direction of the Maremma plain.

The building work for the industrial complex began in 1918 with the creation of a first shaft, Vignaccio II, adjacent to the first washery. In 1955, after a period of transformation and enlargement, a second, larger washery was set up, which remained in use for a decade, up until 1965.

After a long period of disuse in which the plants were dismantled, the complex was completely concealed by mounds of earth and dense vegetation.

In the 1990s a team led by architect Alberto Magnaghi drafted a plan for the mining park of Gavorrano which sought to combine a recovery of the landscape, the restoration of industrial remains, tourist promotion, and the development of the area. The Ravi Marchi washery is located in one of the plots of land that the Municipality of Gavorrano developed according to the suggestions of this plan, drawing upon its own funds and those from the Regional Government of Tuscany. The washery is a unique structure consisting of terraces carved out of the hillside and framed by two slender parallel stone walls. Across five levels, it houses the machinery for grinding the stone, which used to be transported from the new shaft to the summit on a conveyor belt.

The material would then undergo a process of selection from above and be channeled in the form of mud into the big Dor: a large round tank equipped with a floatation system at the foot of the complex.

Linked to the processing of pyrite was a complementary plant for the production of gravel, which was used to fill abandoned underground tunnels and shafts. As a large amount of water had to be employed to process the mineral, the complex is also furnished with storage tanks, located inside a building specifically designed for this purpose.

The roofs, carpentry workshops, lime kilns, explosives depots and all the various other parts of the complex are centered around service areas located at different levels and mutually connected by stairways and ramps.

The most significant aspect of the plan for this open-air museum is the itinerary designed to enable visitors to explore all the various parts of the former industrial complex.

The plan was perfected during the excavation work that was conducted to bring the fully interred areas to light, while ensuring the consolidation and conservation of the walls.

The complex has been treated like an ancient archaeological site.

Jardin des Fonderies

Location: Nantes, France
Plan: 2004–06
Implementation: 2007–09
Ordering party:
SAMOA (Société
d'Aménagement de la
Métropole Ouest
Atlantique)
Project team:
ADH [Doazan +
Hirschberger & associés];
landscape architecture:
Benoîte Doazan, Stéphane
Hirschberger; *technical
and economic consultancy:*
GCA Ingéniérie,
bet structure: BTP;
lighting design: Pixelum
Collaborators:
Elisabeth Salvado, Djamila
Tkoub, Matthieu Pein
Previous use:
Foundry specialized in
manufacturing propellers
for sea liners
Current use: Public garden
Surface: 0.35 ha (0.1 acres)
Cost: 2.2 million euros

The Foundries' Garden is part of a vaster redevelopment project for the Ile de Nantes, that is the transformation of a long unused factory and warehouse district into a large working and housing neighborhood of 350 hectares.
The Foundries' Garden project is located in the middle of the island, far from the Loire River, in a suburban zone with social housing and factories. The project consists in the rehabilitation of the building and public spaces around the Fonderies Atlantique complex. Fonderies Atlantique was a company specialized in manufacturing propellers for sea liners. Many famous liners were equipped with these propellers (*Le France*, *Le Clémenceau*) before the company changed its name and location. Industrial ovens, rails and three pits are visible traces of the old activity that remain on the site.
The main goals were:
- create a "garden under a roof": a covered public space for everyday use, children's games and neighborhood social events (dinners, exhibitions...);
- showcase the former industrial activity, not just as a museum but also as a legacy of a place where many local citizens were employed, worked hard and with passion and for which the conservation of the site is an emotional tribute to the city's industrial past and to their working lives.
The garden is split into two parts:
- "Le jardin des fours," located around the former ovens. Here, *graminaceae*, bamboos and arundos were planted, that create "green columns" next to new water tanks. The garden has become a kind of "machines gallery";
- a "Travels garden" occupies the main part of the site. It's built 1.50 meters above the original ground level because of the polluted soil that needed to be stabilized. The travel theme is illustrated with a collection of plants that came into Europe through the Atlantic ports during the 16th, 17th and 18th centuries. These essences were imported thanks to overseas scientific and economic expeditions and became acclimatized.
The former iron structure was repaired and painted.
The site covering (roof and buildings around) protects it from the wind and allows the temperature in the garden to be 3 or 4 degrees Celsius higher than outside. This "greenhouse's effect" made it possible to plant almost exotic vegetation.
A covered garden needs a complete watering system: rain water is collected by two tanks (2 × 50 cubic meters) and redistributed through different watering networks. Humidity and freshness are maintained by mist spraying the plants.

Des grandes expéditions à ce jardin

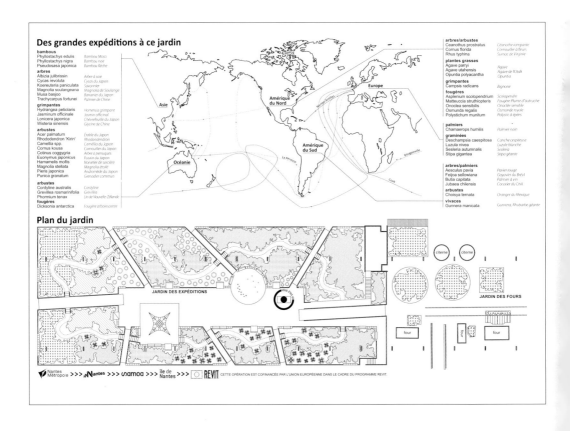

bambous
Phyllostachys edulis — *Bambou Moso*
Phyllostachys nigra — *Bambou noir*
Pseudosasa japonica — *Bambou flèche*

arbres
Albizia julibrissin — *Arbre à soie*
Cycas revoluta — *Cycas du Japon*
Koereuteria paniculata — *Savonnier*
Magnolia soulangeana — *Magnolia de Soulange*
Musa basjoo — *Bananier du Japon*
Trachycarpus fortunei — *Palmier de Chine*

grimpantes
Hydrangea petiolaris — *Hortensia grimpant*
Jasminum officinale — *Jasmin officinal*
Lonicera japonica — *Chèvrefeuille du Japon*
Wisteria sinensis — *Glycine de Chine*

arbustes
Acer palmatum — *Érable du Japon*
Rhododendron 'Kirin' — *Rhododendron*
Camellia spp. — *Camélia du Japon*
Cornus kousa — *Cornouiller du Japon*
Cotinus coggygria — *Arbre à perruques*
Euonymus japonicus — *Fusain du Japon*
Hamamelis mollis — *Noisetier de sorcière*
Magnolia stellata — *Magnolia étoilé*
Pieris japonica — *Andromède du Japon*
Punica granatum — *Grenadier commun*

arbustes
Cordyline australis — *Cordyline*
Grevillea rosmarinifolia — *Grevillea*
Phormium tenax — *Lin de Nouvelle-Zélande*

fougères
Dicksonia antarctica — *Fougère arborescente*

arbres/arbustes
Ceanothus prostratus — *Céanothe rampante*
Cornus florida — *Cornouiller à fleur*
Rhus typhina — *Sumac de Virginie*

plantes grasses
Agave parryi — *Agave*
Agave utahensis — *Agave de l'Utah*
Opuntia polyacantha — *Opuntia*

grimpantes
Campsis radicans — *Bignone*

fougères
Asplenium scolopendrium — *Scolopendre*
Matteuccia struthiopteris — *Fougère Plume d'autruche*
Onoclea sensibilis — *Onoclée sensible*
Osmunda regalis — *Osmonde royale*
Polystichum munitum — *Polystic à épées*

palmiers
Chamaerops humilis — *Palmier nain*

graminées
Deschampsia caespitosa — *Canche cespiteuse*
Luzula nivea — *Luzule blanche*
Sesleria autumnalis — *Seslérie*
Stipa gigantea — *Stipa géante*

arbres/palmiers
Aesculus pavia — *Pavier rouge*
Feijoa sellowiana — *Goyavier du Brésil*
Butia capitata — *Palmier à vin*
Jubaea chilensis — *Cocotier du Chili*

arbustes
Choisya ternata — *Oranger du Mexique*

vivaces
Gunnera manicata — *Gunnera, Rhubarbe géante*

Plan du jardin

The Brick Pit Ring

Location:
Sydney olympic parklands,
Sydney, Australia
Plan: 2004
Implementation: 2005
Ordering party:
Sydney Olympic Park
Authority
Project team:
Neil Durbach, Camilla
Block, David Jaggers, Lisa
Le Van, Joseph Grech
Collaborators:
Complete urban solutions:
Scott Williams (project
manager); *Arups Pty Ltd:*
Tristram Carfrae (structural
engineer); Taylor Thomson
Whitting: Barry Young;
landscape architecture:
Sue Barnsley Design
(Sue Barnsley, Kate
Dewar); *interpretation
soundscape:* CDP Media
(Gary Warner, Peter
Emmett); *color
consultancy:* Virginia
Carroll; *graphic design:*
Eskimo (Art direction
& design); Peter Moore
& Lyndal Harris
(Design & Illustration);
project management:
Andrea Nixon
Ordering party: GMW
Urban: Bob Matchett
Previous use:
Industrial site
Current use:
Public park: Sydney
Olympic Park
Surface:
0.15 ha (0.06 acres)
Cost: 4 million Australian
dollars

The Brick Pit is the last tangible evidence of a vast working industry at Homebush Bay. It is archetypal and primitive, raw, stripped and modified.
The Brick Pit is first a place of extraordinary human endeavor, arrested.
It is a portrait of land disturbance through use. Equally it is a place of adaptation, as an unviable industry is replaced by new sustainable technologies and a refuge for the rare and endangered Green and Golden Bell Frog.
An aerial walkway and outdoor exhibition, twenty meters above the Brick Pit floor, the Ring Walk gives the Brick Pit a genuine urban connection and presence within Sydney Olympic Park. A simple ordering device, the Ring Walk facilitates both access and interpretation to the Brick Pit, while fully recognizing its extremely fragile habitat. The pure form and consistent level of the ring registers the shifting sides and depth of the excavation.

The Ring Walk allows for both the ten-minute walk and a longer layered experience, through widened and shaded sections of the platform. The outside edge of the ring is a variegated screen: part exhibition, mesh and glass viewing panels.
Interlaced with interpretive devices, the ring provides visitors with perspectives into the history of the Brick Pit and its use as a wildlife refuge. The ring has two points of connection to the parklands: one to Australia Avenue and the town center, the other to Marjorie Jackson Drive and the extensive parklands beyond. The steel structure is a slender and delicate intervention within the massive roughness of the pit. A braced cruciform structure comprising a series of improbably thin, flat steel members lightly touchs the base. This attenuated structure appears to tip toe across this fragile site.

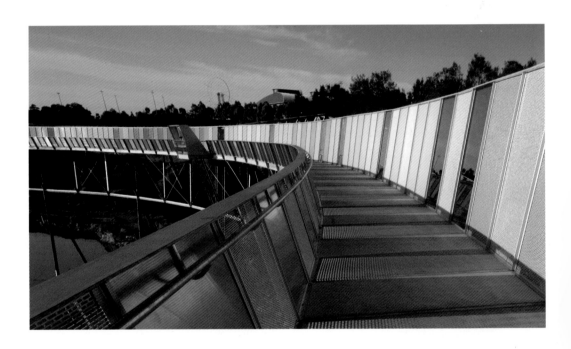

Million Donkey Hotel

Location:
81010 Prata Sannita,
Matese regional park
near Naples, Italy
Plan:
Phase1: 2005;
phase 2: 2006
Implementation:
Phase1: 2005;
phase 2: 2006;
Ordering party:
Paesesaggio workgroup -
Regione Campania
Project team: feld72
Collaborators:
Prata Sannita inhabitants
Previous use:
Urban center
Current use:
Hotel, art village
Surface: 0.03 ha
(0,07 acres)
Cost:
10,000 euros each phase

2005: 73% of the population of Europe lives in cities, and this figure is growing. This percentage doesn't only show the constant growth of (in-between) cities but also and above all the disappearance of the cultural and natural landscapes familiar to us. In a complexity that we possibly are not aware of. The future of these zones, threatened with extinction, is also Europe's future. Migration and its consequences are also the theme of The Million Donkey Hotel, a project by feld72 in the context of the *Villaggio dell'Arte* from the Paesesaggio workgroup.
In August 2005 a group of national and international artists was invited to address questions of identity, territory, social space and landscape in the Matese regional park near Naples by means of art projects involving the participation of the local population. The artists were required to live locally for one month, work together with the local population and draw all materials used from the local villages to stimulate the micro economy of the region.
Prata Sannita is a village divided into two, consisting of a mediaeval *borgo*, known as the Prata Inferiore, which cascades down a hill from a castle, and a newer part, the Prata Superiore, which owes its structure above all to the victory of the motor car and other promises of modernism. In the course of the last century Prata Inferiore was dramatically affected by migration caused by poverty and is now only a small part of the village, inhabited by a minority made up largely of elderly people, and with a very large number of empty buildings, some of which are already in ruins. How could these two clearly separated areas of the village be linked again? How and for whom could the qualities of the almost sculptural spatial landscape be experienced once again? How can spaces that stand for loss become a self-confident part of a new Prata Sannita? How can a "free of" lead to a "free to"?
Prata Sannita is seen in its entirety as a large, scattered hotel that still has rooms available: the abandoned rooms. These are not regarded as bearers of memories

but as potential for the future: they become cells in a larger entity and the entire area of Prata Sannita is perceived as a single action space. The first adaptation of three spatial units (and a special "bathroom") to form "hotel rooms" distanced from everyday life, is a start to making the spaces usable once again, but this time for a nomad not driven by worries about a better future: the traveler. The rooms were alienated and given specific themes and atmospheres based on migration and memory. Through the intervention the local residents were to be stimulated to understand, in a second phase, the other abandoned rooms as further building blocks of this hyper-real hotel and to reactivate them accordingly. The Million Donkey Hotel at the same time became an extension of public space, as in the "off-season" the hotel rooms can also be used by the Prata inhabitants. Through the impressive involvement of up to forty volunteers in the village (an estimated 4300 hours on site) it was possible to implement the Million Donkey Hotel despite the very tight time framework (one month with design practically on site), a low budget (10,000 euros) and the use of only the simplest means. Thanks to the great success, feld72 were invited back the following year. The work in 2006 was focused primarily on public space, for example a ruined house in the immediate proximity of the already-made hotel rooms was converted into a literal "stair-house" (amphitheater), and an association was set up. The Million Donkey Hotel is now run by a small group of "local heroes" who were involved in building it and looks forward to visitors either on site or at www.milliondonkeyhotel.net.

Vacant Lot_ Vacant Lot 1

Location:
Hackney, Tower Hamlets,
Islington, London, UK
Plan: 2007
Implementation: 2007–13
Project team:
What if: projects Ltd
with Groundwork London:
Gareth Morris, Ulrike
Steven (directors)
Collaborators:
Liam Morrisey
Previous use:
Public spaces
Current use:
Agri-civic areas
Surface: 800 lots
in 0.8 hectares (2 acres)
Cost:
300,000 pounds

What if: projects have been mapping vacant and neglected spaces that surround inner city housing estates in London.

Gaps within the urban fabric both detach and isolate communities. The team has been developing a strategy for how these unloved spaces could be appropriated to accommodate the needs of the local population. The basic need for food and outside space for socializing and recreation was developed into a proposal to transform formerly fenced off and neglected pieces of land into allotment gardens. The first Vacant Lot allotment was realized in Shoreditch, East London in 2007. Based on the popularity of this pilot project the scheme was extended to other deprived housing estates in East and North London. The What if team is now working in partnership with a team of four gardeners from Groundwork (environmental charity) to establish twenty new allotment gardens over three years for the production of food on inner city housing estates. Project funding has been secured and various London Boroughs and Housing Associations have confirmed their support. Future allotment gardens are being created with the help of professional gardeners who are going to facilitate training schemes for young people and the engagement of local residents from the culturally diverse communities.

The project is funded by the Big Lottery "Local Food" program and the partnering social housing.

Vacant Lot 1
Location:
Chart Street, London, N1
Implementation: In progress
Ordering party:
Shoreditch Trust as part of the Shoreditch Festival 2007
Project team:
What if: projects Ltd
Surface:
0,03 ha (0,07 acres)
Cost: 6000 pounds

Vacant Lot 1
The first Vacant Lot allotment garden was started in May 2007 with the construction of a water tower that projects above the boundary walls of the site and announces a small change to this inner city housing area in Shoreditch. Flyers were distributed to the surrounding housing, inviting residents to become involved and take ownership of a 1-square-meter plot of land. With the help of the local community a total of 70.5 tonne bulk bags were subsequently arranged and filled with soil to form the allotment space.

The building process, together with the distribution of flyers and a newsletter, attracted many residents to become part of the project. Sixty-three interested households from the surrounding housing estates were given ownership of a Vacant Lot plot and were handed a key to the gate for a one-off fee of 3.50 pounds. Since June 2007 local residents are carefully tending a spectacular array of vegetables, salads, fruit and flowers in their individual plots. As well as the local community, insects and birds have moved in and thrive in this new natural habitat. Plot holders take care of their individual plots and tend to visit the garden on a regular basis to sow, water their plants and to collect their harvest. Produce during the first two years included tomatoes, a variety of salads, beetroot, spinach, radishes, courgette, cucumber, carrots, different kinds of beans, corn, cabbage, peppers, squash, potatoes, herbs, strawberries and flowers.

The Vacant Lot has become a space for meeting neighbors, BBQs', sitting in the sun, playing and gardening. Plot holders of different age groups and cultural backgrounds meet, exchange food, seeds and gardening advice. A new sense of community has emerged.

Sixty Minute Man

Location:
Biennale 2000, Venice, Italy
Plan: 2000
Implementation: 2000
Ordering party:
La Biennale di Venezia
Project team: Sami Rintala
Previous use:
Freight barge
Current use: Public garden
Surface:
34 m × 7 m × 5.5 m
(37 yd × 7.7 yd × 6 yd)

An archaic oak park was planted inside a 34-meter-long freight barge, which was found out of use in the Laguna of Venice. The park is growing on top of 60 minutes' worth of composted human waste from the city of Venice. The ship was taken to the Arsenale harbor and opened as a public park, commenting on the Biennale theme "Less aesthetics, more ethics."
The rusting freight barge *Topogigio* was found filled with mud and dirt at the port of Chioggia, out of use, but still floating. The vessel was cleaned and the necessary openigs were cut in order to create a series of spaces. The gangways from the quay up to the boat and down to the cargo space are made out of iron elements, used in Venice for reinforcing the islands.
The twenty-four oaks planted on the human waste symbolize the simple way of living and the eternal circulation of organic material. The leaf crowns are partly visible from the quay, but one can not see the park itself until you climb a gangway to the deck of the barge. From there, you descend another ramp into the trees.
All the material is recycled—put together to create an architectonic collage.
The oaks would have a full lifetime with the energy of the human waste produced by venetians in one hour.

Glossary*

Metamorphosis
Latin, from Greek
metamorph sis, from
metamorphoun to
transform, from *meta +
morph* form
First known use: 1533

- change of physical form,
structure, or substance
especially by supernatural
means
- striking alteration
in appearance, character,
or circumstances
- a typically marked
and more or less abrupt
developmental change
in the form or structure
of an animal (as a butterfly
or a frog) occurring
subsequent to birth
or hatching

In biology, any striking
developmental change of
an animal's form or
structure, accompanied by
physiological, biochemical,
and behavioral changes.
The best-known
examples occur among
insects, which
may exhibit complete
or incomplete
metamorphosis
(*see* nymph).
The complete
metamorphosis
of butterflies, moths,
and some other insects
involves four stages: egg,
larva (caterpillar), pupa
(chrysalis or cocoon),
and adult. The change
from tadpole to frog is
an example of
metamorphosis among
amphibians; some
echinoderms,
crustaceans, mollusks,
and tunicates also
undergo metamorphosis.

Mutation
First known use:
14th century

- a significant and basic
alteration: change
- a relatively permanent
change in hereditary
material involving either
a physical change
in chromosome relations
or a biochemical change
in the codons that make
up genes; *also:* the
process of producing
a mutation
- an individual, strain,
or trait resulting
from mutation

Alteration in the genetic
material of a cell that is
transmitted to the cell's
offspring. Mutations may
be spontaneous or
induced by outside
factors (mutagens).
They take place in the
genes, occurring when
one base is substituted
for another in the
sequence of bases that
determines the genetic
code, or when one
or more bases are
inserted or deleted from
a gene. Many mutations
are harmless, often
masked by the presence
of a dominant normal
gene (*see* dominance).
Some have serious
consequences; for
example, a particular

mutation inherited from
both parents results
in sickle-cell anemia.
Only mutations that occur
in the sex cells (eggs
or sperm) can be
transmitted to the
individual's offspring.
Alterations caused by
these mutations are
usually harmful. In the
rare instances in which
a mutation produces
a beneficial change,
the percentage of
organisms with this gene
will tend to increase until
the mutated gene
becomes the norm in the
population. In this way,
beneficial mutations
serve as the raw material
of evolution.

Prosthetic
First known use:
circa 1890

- of, relating to, or being
a prosthesis
<a *prosthetic*device> <pr
osthetic limbs>; *also:* of
or relating to
prosthetics <*prosthetic*
research>

Prosthesis
New Latin, from Greek,
addition, from
prostithenai to add to,
from *pros-* in addition
to + *tithenai* to put
First known use: circa
1900

- an artificial device to
replace or augment a
missing or impaired part
of the body

Artificial substitute for a missing part of the body, usually an arm or leg. Prostheses have evolved from wooden legs and hooks that replaced hands to sophisticated plastic, fibreglass, and metal devices designed to fit limbs amputated at different points. They may have working joints and allow motion either by amplification of electric current generated by muscle contractions or by actual attachment to the muscles. Arm prostheses usually allow some degree of grasping and manipulation. External or implanted breast prostheses are used after mastectomy.

Rebirth
First known use: 1837

- a period in which something becomes popular again after a long period of time when it was not popular
- a period of new life, growth or activity

Rebuild
First known use: 1537

- to build (something) again after it has been damaged or destroyed
- to make important improvements or changes in (something)
- to make extensive repairs to: reconstruct <*rebuild* a war-torn city>

- to restore to a previous state <*rebuild* inventories

Recovery
First known use: 15th century

- the act or process of becoming healthy after an illness or injury: the act or process of recovering
- the act or process of returning to a normal state after a period of difficulty
- the return of something that has been lost, stolen, etc.

Recycle
First known use: 1925

- to pass again through a series of changes or treatments
- to process (as liquid body waste, glass, or cans) in order to regain material for human use
- to reuse or make (a substance) available for reuse for biological activities through natural processes of biochemical degradation or modification <green plants *recycling* the residue of forest fires> <*recycle* ADP back to ATP>
- to adapt to a new use: alter
- to bring back: reuse <*recycles* a number of good anecdotes>
- to make ready for reuse <a plan

to *recycle* vacant tenements>

Regeneration
First known use: 14th century

- an act or the process of regenerating: the state of being regenerated
- spiritual renewal or revival
- the renewal, re-growth, or restoration of a body or a bodily part, tissue, or substance after injury or as a normal bodily process <continual *regen eration* of epithelial cells> <*regeneration* of the uterine lining>— compare regulation

Renewal
First known use: circa 1686

- the act of extending the period of time when something is effective or valid: the act of renewing something
- the state of being made new, fresh or strong again: the state of being renewed
- the rebuilding of a large area (as of a city) by a public authority

Reuse
First known use: 1843

- to use again especially in a different way or after reclaiming or reprocessing <the need to *reuse* scarce

resources> <*reuse* packing material as insulation>

Salvage
French, from Middle French, from *salver* to save
First known use: 1645

- compensation paid for saving a ship or its cargo from the perils of the sea or for the lives and property rescued in a wreck
- the act of saving or rescuing a ship or its cargo
- the act of saving or rescuing property in danger (as from fire)
- property saved from destruction in a calamity (as a wreck or fire)
- something extracted (as from rubbish) as valuable or useful

Selection
First known use: circa 1623

- the act of choosing something or someone from a group
- someone or something that is chosen from a group
- a collection of things chosen from a group of similar things

In biology, the preferential survival and reproduction or preferential elimination of individuals with certain genotypes, by means

of natural or artificial
controlling factors.
The theory of evolution
by natural selection was
proposed by Charles
Darwin and Alfred Russel
Wallace in 1858. Artificial
selection differs from
natural selection in that
inherited variations in a
species are manipulated
by humans through
controlled breeding
in order to create
qualities economically
or aesthetically desirable
to humans, rather than
useful to the organism in
its natural environment.

*Definitions based on
Merriam-webster.com

ADH [Doazan + Hirschberger & Associés], is an architectural, urban planning and landscape design practice that was founded in 1996 by Benoîte Doazan and Stéphane Hirschberger. They were joined by two additional partners in 2010: Nicolas Novello and Yves Le Jallé. The agency develops a cross-cutting activity and works on projects of various scales and stakes. Stéphane Hirschberger has been a teacher at the ensapBx (École Nationale Supérieure d'Architecture et de Paysage de Bordeaux) since 2004. The firm—the Maison des danses, Bordeaux, and Moirax cultural center are among its projects—won the competition for the redevelpment of Place Ravezies, and is currently working on Circus Arts, Auch and the Soulac promenade.

Established in Lille in 1982 by Sébastien Giorgis, **Agence Paysages** is a co-operative Landscape Architecture agency that currently employs eight people. The studio is specialized in the design of exterior spaces, from gardens and urban spaces to the redevelopment of brownfield sites, utilizing a broad-ranging skills in botany, hydrology, geology and ecology, coupled with knowledge drawn from materials science, history and sociology.

Agence Ter was set up in 1986 by three landscape architects: Henri Bava, Michel Hoessler e Olivier Philippe—all of whom trained at the Ecole Nationale Superieure du Paysage in Versailles, or at the Ecole Superieure d'Architecture des Jardins et du Paysage in Paris. The practice was awarded the Silver medal of Académie Francaise d'Architecture in 2008.

Aldayjover arquitectura y paisaje is an architecture office founded in 1996. It is formed by two partners, Iñaki Alday and Margarita Jover. The firm was awarded the FAD Award (2009), the European Prize for Urban Public Space (2002) and García Mercadal Award (2001 and 2005), besides being a finalist in the Spanish Architecture Biennial (2005 and 2009) or the Ibero-American Architecture Biennial (2004).

Since 1999 **AllesWirdGut** has been working on projects on different scales: from the development of urban systems to the planning of interiors. The studio follows a dynamic approach, seeking to make the most of the potential of each context. By approaching problems as opportunities for planning, new and unexpected architectural possibilities are brought out. The chief aim of the studio is to find and express added qualities, based on the targeted questions for each commission. AllesWirdGut focuses on contents and possible synergies: on the integration of methods that make possible solutions cost-efficient.

Jean-Charles-Adolphe **Alphand** (1817–1891), engineer of the Ecole Nationale des Ponts et Chaussées since 1857 and Director of Public Works since 1867, was invited to contribute to the "grands travaux" carried out in Paris between 1854 and 1891. Horticulturalist Pierre **Barillet-Deschamps** (1824–1873) is the leading interpreter of the Haussmann garden model. The head gardener of the Service de Promenade et Plantations de la Ville de Paris, he designed the main gardens and parks in 19th-century Paris. Architect Gabriel **Davioud** (1824–1881) was inspector general for architectural works in Paris, and chief architect for its parks and public gardens.

Established in Milan in 2004, **Alterazioni Video** is a collective of five artists (Paololuca Barbieri Marchi, Andrea Masu, Alberto Caffarelli, Giacomo Porfiri and Matteo Erenbourg) based in Milan, Berlin and New York. The collective acts as an international network, geographically dispersed and mobile, and focuses on issues of disinformation and the relations between truth and representation, legality and illegality, freedom and censorship, mingling art with political activism across a range of different fields: architecture, cooking, agriculture, anthropology, contemporary art, and village fairs.

AMD&ART is a non-profit organization that is "artfully transforming environmental liabilities into community assets." The AMD&ART process is one that combines public art, environmental improvement and community engagement in treating acid mine drainage (AMD), an emblem of regional social and economic woes. With multidisciplinary intervention and wide public participation, AMD&ART has created a holistic approach to re-creating place, incorporating recreational elements, artful spaces, educational opportunities, historic reminders and restored wildlife habitat into designs for passive AMD treatment systems.

Tadao Ando, born in 1941, is one of the most renowned contemporary Japanese architects. He is an honorary member of the American Institute of Architects, the American Academy of Arts and Letters, as well as the Royal Academy of Arts in London. He was also a visiting professor at Yale, Columbia, UC Barkley, and Harvard Universities.

Studio Anzani has been working in the field of architectural and urban planning since 1983, also focusing on landscape planning and enhancement, both on a local scale and a wider one. This work has been combined with research activity and the teaching of undergraduate and master courses in the universities of Naples, Camerino and Salerno, and for other cultural institutions, both in Italy and abroad.

The **Hong Kong Architectural Services Department** ensures the quality and sustainable

development of community facilities, the quality upkeep of community facilities, provides quality professional advisory services on community facilities and related matters, promotes best practices in the building industry.

Established by **Shlomo Aronson** in 1969, the office is active in the fields of architecture, landscape architecture and urban design; throughout the years the office was involved in hundreds of projects in Israel and around the world, ranging from small scaled urban plazas and parks, transportation projects to master plans on a national scale. 2012: Shlomo Aronson is awarded the Yakir Yerushalayim Prize - Worthy Citizenship of Jerusalem by the city of Jerusalem 2012; winner of the Ot Ha'itzuv Municipality Design Competition with Park HaHurshot Project in Tel Aviv. 2011: Shlomo Aronson Architects wins the Global Award for Sustainable Architecture 2011.

The two architects who designed Skogskyrkogården, **Gunnar Asplund and Sigurd Lewerentz**, met as students and crossed

paths several times over the years. When the Cemetery Committee announced an international competition to design Skogskyrkogården, they decided to produce their own entry together. This entry, Tallum, won the competition and work started a year or so later. Together they created a unity of landscaping and buildings that has become one of the world's leading architectural sites. Lewerentz was responsible for much of the landscaping. He also designed the classicist Chapel of Resurrection in the southern part of Skogskyrkogården.

Batlle i Roig, Arquitectes is an architecture office, formed since 1981 by Enric Batlle and Joan Roig and located in Esplugues de Llobregat (Barcelona). Enric Batllle (Barcelona, 1956) is Doctor Architect and teacher at the Department of Urbanism and Land management in the ETSA Vallès (Architecture School). Joan Roig (Barcelona, 1954) is an architect and has taught many years in the ETSA Barcelona (Architecture School), part of the Department of Architectural Projects, as well as at the Master of Landscape Architecture and in many international Architecture schools.

Massimo Carmassi was born in Pisa in 1943. Professor of Architectural and Urban Planning at the IUAV University of Venice, he has taught Architectural Planning in the faculties of Architecture of the universities of Ferrara, Genoa, Turin and Reggio Calabria, as well as at the Accademia di Architettura di Mendrisio, Hochschule der Kunst in Berlin, and at Syracuse University (New York). The founder and director of the Project Office of the city of Pisa between 1974 and 1990, he currently exercises his profession in the studio he operates in Florence, focusing on restoration and new architecture.

Sami Rintala (born 1969) is an architect and an artist, with a long merit list after finishing his architect studies in Helsinki, Finland in 1999. He established the architect office **Casagrande & Rintala** in 1998, which produced a series of acknowledged architectural installations around the world during the next five years until 2003. In 2008, Rintala started a new architect office with Icelandic architect Dagur Eggertsson, called Rintala Eggertsson Architects. The office is based in Oslo, South Norway and Bodø, North Norway.

James Corner Field Operations is an international landscape architecture, urban design and planning practice based in New York City. Major design projects include the High Line, New York; the 890-hectare Fresh Kills Park, Staten Island; the 1800-hectare Shelby Farms Park, Memphis; the 35-kilometer-long Atlanta Beltline, Georgia; the Aria Pool Deck and Gardens, City Center, Las Vegas; and the Palisades Gardens, Santa Monica. The work of the practice has been published and exhibited internationally, including the Venice Biennale, the Lisbon Triennale, the New York Museum of Modern Art and the National Design Museum.

Pascal Cribier—born in Normandy in 1953—has been a state-registered architect since 1978 and a state-registered landscape architect since 1982. He has designed public parks and private gardens (Tuileries, Méry–sur-Oise, Aramon, Woolton, Montana, Bora Bora…) and partecipated in urban plans and projects with Patrick Ecoutin in Lyons, Nicolas Michelin in Lille-Sud, and Djamel Klouche in Fives. Cribier is a member of the consulting commission for the Grand Paris project.

DeSo was founded by Olivier Souquet and François Defrain in 2005. DeSo creates public buildings, offices, urban projects and residential buildings. Olivier Souquet and François Defrain are AFEX members. Christine Dalnoky is D.P.L.G. landscape architect, a graduate of the Académie de France in Rome 1987–88 and Silver medal from the Académie d'Architecture in 2000. She was awarded at the Barcelona Biennial of Landscape Architecture in 2001. She has worked with architects the likes of Renzo Piano, Norman Foster, Richard Rogers, Gilles Perraudin, Jean-Marie Duthilleul, Paul Andreu, Jean Nouvel, and Bruno Fortier. She is Professor at the Istituto di Architettura di Mendrisio (Canton Ticino, Switzerland) and lecturer at the Istituto Universitario di Architettura di Venezia.

Diller Scofidio + Renfro is an interdisciplinary design studio based in New York City with an approach that straddles design, the visual arts, and the performing arts. James Corner is a registered landscape architect and urban designer, and founder and director of James Corner Field Operations, where he oversees the production of all design projects in the office. He is also professor of Landscape Architecture at the University of Pennsylvania, School of Design. He was educated at Manchester Metropolitan University, England, and University of Pennsylvania.

D.I.R.T. studio (Dump It Right There) was founded in 1992 by Julie Bargmann as a critical, design research-based practice. D.I.R.T. studio operates out of a love for the landscape, a concern for marginalized communities and an obsession with urban The studio is inspired to remake fallow and derelict terrain into renewed landscapes of ecological and cultural production.

The studio is managed by Neil **Durbach** and Camilla **Block**, and David Jaggers. Their work is recognised as both iconic and innovative through international publications and awards. Most recently DBJ won the 2010 AIA Sir Aurthur G. Stephenson Award for Commercial Architecture (NSW) for Roslyn Street, the AIA Sir Osborn McCutcheon Award for Commercial Architecture (VIC) for Sussan Sportsgirl Headquarters in 2009

and the RAIA Llyod Rees Civic Design Award (NSW) and RAIA National Special Jury Award for the Brick Pit Ring in 2006.

feld72 is a collective, a laboratory for architecture, engaged in research and finding new strategies for cliché-dominated or underestimated (urban) conditions. feld72 continuously focuses on the borderline where one system converts into another. How can you re-program the ways people use spaces and how they respond to social rules? Possible answers vary from object-related planning to urban investigations and interventions.

The **GrünBerlin GmbH** is a service company of the City of Berlin for the development of urban open space. For more than thirty years it has been in charge of a great number of outstanding green projects in Berlin. As such it plans, develops, realizes, maintains and operates parks of different size (altogether about 250 hectares) and various characters.

Markus Gnüchtel and Michael Triebswetter founded **GTL Gnüchtel - Triebswetter Landscape Architects** in 1991 in

Kassel. GTL is also active in China, where there is a representative office in Beijing, starting 2005. In 2007 the opening of a further location followed in Düsseldorf. Participating in numerous competitions gives the office the opportunity to constantly break new grounds in conceptual thinking and in the final realization and presentation of its design ideas.

Eduardo Chillida (1920–2002) is a Spanish sculptor. In 1958 he was awarded the Grand Prize for Sculpture at the Venice Biennale. Two years later he received the Kandinsky-Prize and in 1980 the New York Guggenheim Museum showed a retrospective of his oeuvre.
Estudio Guadiana is an architecture practice established by José A. Fernández-Ordóñez and Lorenzo Fernández-Ordóñez in 1997.

Martine Guiton is a state-registered architect and landscape developer (specialized in the field of hydraulics).
Main assignments and projects:
- Landscape architect for the new city of Marne-la-Vallée (1980–82): person in charge of reforesting and the planting of rows of trees.

- Appointed landscape architect of the EDF (Electricité de France) (1982–2000): in charge of tree-planning, reforestation and the development of ponds for large power stations, as well as teaching engineers about issues related to planted areas.
- Lecturer in Landscaping and person in charge of courses on flooding risks and means of landscape protection (such as the creation of retention basins) at the École du Paysage in Versailles (1986–96), École d'Horticulture in Angers, and École Nationale des Ponts et Chaussées and University of Jussieu in Paris.

The **Richard Haag Associates** studio was established in 1961. Many of the projects it has completed are large-scale ones: public parks, cultural centers, university campuses, and museums. Sensitivity to the natural environment and an interest in the reuse of existing structures are the foundations of the philosophy of the studio, which has found concrete expression through over 500 projects.

Barbara Holzer and Tristan Kobler have been jointly running the firm **Holzer Kobler Architekturen** since 2004, and have

successfully realized international projects. Awards: 2013, German Façade Prize Nomination for paläon, research and experience centre Schöningen Spears, Schöningen, Germany; Iconic Awards; Winner category Architecture Event/Exhibition with Sasso San Gottardo; AIT Award. 2012: Selection Public Buildings, Interior: Collections Gallery History of Switzerland, Focus Terra; Selection Conversion: Realstadt. Wishes knocking on realitiy's doors. 2011: Design Prize Switzerland: Nomination with Realstadt; Nomination with 2000 Watt Gesellschaf.

The **IBA Association**, supported by four rural districts in Brandenburg as well as the city of Cottbus and promoted by the Brandenburg Land, is the heart of a network connecting the people involved on site with each other and with national and international experts by means of a planning-related target. IBA combines creative and technical innovation, confronts science and arts with this objective, draws international attention to the region— and thus creates regional circular economy flows as well as new jobs.

Ilex was founded by Martine Rascle and Guerric Péré in 1987. It is formed by a group of landscape designers and architects specialized in the planning of exteriors and the supervision of projects on any scale. Ilex, represented by Guerric Péré and JeanClaude Durual, directs its personal urban concept towards horizons that differ from those of a simple functional and spacial composition, with an approach that is at the same time pragmatic and creative. Guerric Péré teaches in the Marseilles branch of the École Nationale Supérieure du Paysage of Versailles (ENSP).

Sylvia Karres and Bart Brands founded **Karres and Brands Landscape Architects** in 1997. Since then the firm has worked on a wide variety of projects, studies and design competitions in the Netherlands and internationally.

Büro Kiefer was founded in Berlin by Gabriele G. Kiefer in 1989, just before the fall of the Berlin wall. Combining both a mathematic and aesthetic logic, Büro Kiefer's work responds to the ever-expanding responsibilities of landscape design: interaction with the fields of architecture, urban and regional development, and even the cultural tradition of garden art.

Rosa Grena Kliass Arquitetura Paisagística Planejamento e Projetos Ltda. was founded in 1970. A group of landscape architects has been supported by the collaboration of special professionals as architects, urban planners, designers, engineers, botanists, phytogeographists, pedologists, geomorphologists, climatologists, hydrologists, lawyers and managers.
The firm has received commissions by private enterprises as well as governmental authorities and has proved a pioneer in many projects in which it has introduced new working methodologies.

Laetitia **Lara**, sculptor and architect, is the founder of the association and has been at the head of the overall project from the start, as person in charge of its general supervision and coordination. Austín Petschen, architect, is the cosignatory (together with Laetitia Lara) of the architectural projects developed between 1997 and 2009, and the designer of the information pavilion.
Virginia Pallarés, architect,

has been working with Laetitia Lara on the architectural projects since 2009. José Bravo, landscape gardener, has designed the *Laberint dels vergers* (Garden Labyrinth), the framework for all the reclamation/regeneration work on green areas and the creation of gardens.

Bernard Lassus graduated from the Ecole Nationale Supérieure des Beaux-Arts in Paris and received his training in Fernand Léger's atelier. He soon emerged as one of the leading landscape designers in Europe and one of the founders of French landscaping.
In 1996 Lassus was awarded the Grand Prix National du Paysage; in 2002 he received an honorary degree from Montreal University, in 2006 from Hannover University, and in 2007 from Venice University. Since 1991 Lassus has served as an advisor for the Direction des Routes du Ministère de l'Equipement of the French government. He has designed motorway rest areas and has developed the landscape plan for the Chamonix-Tunnel du Mont Blanc exit.
In 2005 he received the title of Chevalier de la Légion d'honneur from the French government.

Latitude Nord, a landscape design studio, was founded in 1981 by Gilles Vexlard and Laurence Vacherot. The studio is specialized in urban planning and the implementation of projects for large spaces and landscapes, with plans for the design and development of urban realities on different scales and various contexts (sports facilities, lyceums, schools, urban gardens, etc.).
Among the awards received by Latitude Nord, the International Urban Landscape Award in 2006 and the Grand Prix National du Paysage for the recreational park of Le Port aux Cerises à Draveil (Essonne) in 2009.

LIN was founded in 2001 by Finn Geipel and Giulia Andi. It is an agency for architecture and urbanism, based in Berlin and Paris. LIN develops singular architectural projects as well as urban and landscape projects. Flexibility, open programming and the reduction of resource consumption are recurring issues.
The method may best be described as an integrative approach. A team of consultants from different fields participate in our projects (structure, climatic conception, light, philosophy, art, design,

information design, architecture theory, landscape, ecology, urban economy). LIA (Laboratory for Integrative Architecture), located at Berlin University, is the office's permanent research platform.

The **Nowa** studio was established in 2005. The studio operates in different fields: from integrated architectural planning to project management, from feasibility studies to environmental and landscape consultancy. The studio also focuses on the organizing of workshops, the hosting of exhibitions, and editing of books and catalogues. It is currently engaged in a number of both public and private planning projects.

Dominique Perrault received many prestigious prizes and awards, including the AFEX Award for the Ewha Woman's University in Korea and the Grande Médaille d'or d'Architecture in 2010, the Mies van der Rohe prize in 1997 and the Grand prix national de l'architecture in 1993. The body of his work was assembled in a solo exhibition: "Dominique Perrault Architecture," held at the Centre Georges Pompidou in Paris in 2008 and subsequently moved to Madrid and Tokyo.

Gustafson Porter is an International Landscape Design practice based in London. The practice operates across the diverse disciplines of landscape, architecture, engineering and design. The work expresses the tension and balance between opposing forces in the built and natural worlds, with bold contemporary designs. The form's approach is inspired by the complexity of the human condition and the desire for stability as well as change in modern world. Our approach is simultaneously rational and emotional, disciplined and relaxed, structured yet ever changing.

Tanya Preminger is a multimedia artist and designer who, amongst other disciplines, works in the fields of Landscape Art, Environmental Art and Ecological Art. Tanya was born in the USSR and graduated from the Surikov Academy of Art in Moscow, with an MA degree. Today she lives in Israel. Over the years she has participated in many international competitions and symposiums and placed numerous works in Europe, the Americas and the Far East.

President of the Fondazione Fiumara d'Arte, **Antonio Presti** was born in Messina on 12 May 1957. In 1982 he established the Associazione Culturale Fiumara d'Arte. A Construction Engineering student at Palermo University; following the death of his father he quit his studies to take over his family's business: a well-established company based in Castel di Tusa and specialized in the manufacture of road material. At the age of 29 he chose to fully pursue his vocation as an "artist," making art and ethics the two guiding lines for all his choices. To commemorate his father, he designed an artistic itinerary evoking a sense of continuity between life and death, as a symbol of the preservation of memory through contemporary art.

PROAP brings together a large number of architects, landscape architects, and designers. The core group is headed by João Nunes and Carlos Ribas. The studio's work and research conform to the principle of operating upon the landscape by acknowledging and interpreting its underlying laws and mechanisms.

The **Rehabilitation Inspection and Compliance Section of the Ministry of Northern Development, Mines and Forestry** (**MNDMF**) is responsible for ensuring that all mine sites—both operating and abandoned mines—are rehabilitated in compliance with the requirements of Ontario's Mining Act. The rehabilitation of the highest priority, Crown-held sites, is conducted under the Abandoned Mines Rehabilitation Program (AMRP). Since this program began in 1999, 98 million dollars have been spent on the rehabilitation of more than seventy-five abandoned mine sites across Ontario, including the Kam Kotia Mine site.

Rehwaldt Landschaftsarchitekten was founded in 1993 by Till Rehwaldt in Dresden. Main sectors of the studio's working method are public open space planning, recreation and leisure facilities as well as urban planning. The practice works in two offices and on thematically and regionally multifaceted projects. Participation in design competitions is a recurring challenge and many projects have been acquired in this way.

Bernardo **Secchi** and Paola **Viganò** founded their studio in 1990. Since then, they have won several international competitions (among the realized projects: the Spoor Noord Park and Theaterplein in Antwerp, a system of public spaces in Mechelen, the cemetery in Courtrai, the public spaces in La Courrouze, Rennes, etc.). The practice is today working on different projects in Europe (Zac Courrouze in Rennes, Galgenwel Park and New South Master Plan in Antwerp, etc.). In 2009 Secchi and Viganò were among the ten teams selected for the "Grand Paris project" and in 2012 for "New Moscow."

Eduardo Souto de Moura graduated in Architecture at Porto in 1980. Between 1974 and 1979 he worked in architect Álvaro Siza's studio. Between 1981 and 1991 he was Assistant Professor in the Architecture Faculty of the University of Porto. He is Visiting Professor at the universities of Belleville in Paris, Harvard, Dublin, Zurich and Lausanne. He has held seminars in the most important faculties around the world and his works have been on display in Portugal,

France, Italy and the United States.
In 1999 he received an Honorable mention in the Stone in Architecture awards for his Pousada Santa Maria do Bouro and the FAD Critics Award for his cultural center in Matosinhos.

The project was developed by a transatlantic team, based in Italy and the USA, formed by Elisabetta Terragni (**Studio Terragni Architetti**; installation and architecture), Jeffrey T. Schnapp (Stanford Humanities Lab; project director and curator- in-chief); FilmWork (production and multimedia); Gruppe Gut (graphics).
Elisabetta Terragni has been running her Como-based studio since 2001. After graduating at the Milan Polytechnic, she was an assistant at the Zuyrich Polytechnic, spent two years in Montreal and, back to Milan, taught Museography at the Polytechnic. In 2005–06 Terragni was Distinguished Visiting Professor at the New York Institute of Technology and currently is Associate Professor at the City University of New York.

Topotek 1 is a landscape architecture studio that specializes in the design and construction of unique urban open spaces. Founded by Martin Rein-Cano in 1996, the studio's roster of German and international projects has ranged in scale from the Master Plan to the private garden. Each project strives to respond to site conditions and programmatic necessities with a compelling concept, high quality of design and efficient implementation.

Turenscape is an internationally awarded multidisciplinary firm founded by Doctor Kongjian Yu. "Nature, Man and Spirits as One" is the philosophy underlying all of Turenscape's designs. It employs 500 professionals who work as an integrated team in architecture, landscape architecture, urban planning and design. Turenscape's projects have earned worldwide recognition for innovative and environmentally sound designs, including eight ASLA Awards, and seven other honor awards, 2009 ULI Global Award for Excellence, four Water front Awards of Excellence; World's Best Landscape Award of the World Architecture Festival.

Michael **Van Valkenburgh Associates** (MVVA) is engaged in design and planning as a creative collective. The firm is guided by principals Laura Solano, Matthew Urbanski, Paul Seck, Gullivar Shepard, and Michael Van Valkenburgh. Their projects have received numerous honors, including awards from the American Society of Landscape Architects, the American Planning Association, the U.S. National Park Service, the Municipal Arts Society of New York City, the Royal Architecture Institute of Canada, the Institute of Transportation Engineers, the Building Stone Institute, the Waterfront Center, Places/EDRA, Progressive Architecture, and the National Trust for Historic Preservation.

Weiss/Manfredi Architecture/Landscape/Urbanism is a multidisciplinary design practice based in New York City known for their integration of architecture, art, infrastructure, and landscape design. Weiss/Manfredi received the Academy Award in Architecture, an award given annually by the American Academy of Arts and Letters, acknowledging the distinct vision of the firm. They were also named one of North America's "Emerging Voices" by the Architectural League of New York and the firm won the New York City AIA Gold Medal of Honor.

Founded in 1982, **Wenk Associates** is specialized in urban planning and landscape architectural services. The studio is recognized nationally and internationally for integration of natural systems and processes into urban settings; and for transforming degraded landscapes into vibrant public or natural realms.

What if: projects work focuses on urban sustainability and new ways of implementing ideas and strategies through engaging communities.
The value of the land is seen as a place for humanity to re-connect with nature. In this way the natural qualities of the site become a catalyst for regeneration of the surrounding area. Over the past few years we have initiated and realized various site-specific projects that are responsive to culturally diverse inner city neighborhoods.

Photo References

Hong Kong Wetland Park, Agriculture, Fisheries and Conservation Department of the Hong Kong SAR Government: pp. 88, 89, 90-91
© Queen's Printer for Ontario, 2010: pp. 43, 44, 45
© Hervé Abbadie: pp. 242, 245
© ALBATROSS photography Israel: p. 39
© Bellingroth: p. 124 (left)
© Brett Boardman: p. 249
© Horst Burger: p. 123 (bottom)
© Kraig Carlstrom: p. 248
© Michel Denancé/DPA/adagp/by Siae 2014: p. 40 (right)
© DeSo-Defrain-Souquet architectes: pp. 207, 208-209
© DPA/Adagp/ by SIAE 2014: pp. 40 (left), 41
© Rob Feenstra: p. 151
© LIN Finn Geipel + Giulia Andi-Christian Richters: p. 235 (top), 237
© GrünBerlin GmbH: pp. 124-125 a destra
© Susanne Hallmann, Cemeteries Administration of the City of Stockholm: p. 57
© Hertha Hurnaus: pp. 214, 216-217, 250, 251
© Hanns Joosten. p. 135
© Holger Koppatsch: pp. 126-127, 128, 129
© Kongjian Yu / Turenscape: pp. 140, 141, 142-143, 144-145
© Bernard Lassus: pp. 146, 147, 148-149
© Latitude Nord: p. 123 (top)

© Fotag Luftbild – MRG: p. 121 (top)
© Tanya Preminger: p. 53
© Rainer Schmidt: p. 122
© Roger de Souza: p. 247
© Marieke Wiersma: p. 150

Agence Pasyages: pp. 130, 131, 132, 133
Agence Ter: p. 78
AMD&ART, Inc., N.P: pp. 138, 139
TADAO ANDO ARCHITECT & ASSOCIATES: pp. 68, 69, 70-71
Iwan Baan © 2009: pp. 172, 174-175
Luca Babini, Gabriele Basilico:pp. 33, 34, 35
D.I.R.T. studio: pp. 199, 200-201
Benjamin Benschneider: pp. 203, 204
Luftbild Bonames: p. 181 (top)
Hans Blossey: p. 79 (bottom)
Hilary Casey Inchingolo: pp. 208-209
Mario Ciampi: pp. 240, 241
Stephan Cop, Frankfurt am Main: pp. 181 (bottom), 182-183
Teresa Cos: pp. 116-117
Pascal Cribier: pp. 165, 166, 167
Pierluigi Faggion: pp. 232, 233
Elizabeth Felicella: p. 213 (top)
Luis Ferriera Alves: pp. 224, 227
Fiumara d'Arte: p. 119
GBSL e. V: p. 86
GBSL: p. 87
Steven Geeraerd: p. 114

Salvatore Gozzo: pp. 177, 178, 179
IBA Rainer Weisflog: p. 23 (bottom)
Rosa Grena Kliass APPP Ltda.: p. 10
Martine Guiton: pp. 102, 103, 104, 105
Richard Haag: pp. 160 (left), 161, 162-163
Richard Haag Associates: pp. 26, 27, 161 (right)
Holzer Kobler - Paco Carrascosa: pp. 238, 239
Nelson Kon: pp. 110, 111, 112- 113
Jan-Oliver Kunze, LIN: p. 222
Illustration © LIN: p. 236
Alex MacLean, Landslides Photography: p. 190
Laurie Olin: p. 157
Planergruppe Oberhausen: p. 79 (top), 81
Photo Daniel Diaz Font: p. 55
Photo IBA_Aris Tsantiropoulos: p. 18
Photo IBA_Frank Döring: p. 25
Photo illustration courtesy of © Shlomo Aronson Architects: pp. 36, 37, 38
Photo: Thomas Kläber: p. 22
Photo: Profifoto Kliche: p. 23 (top)
Photo: Michael Klug: p. 224
Photo: Radke, LMBV: p. 21
Photo Jesús Uriarte: p. 54 (bottom)
Photos Courtesy of Wenk Associates, Inc: pp. 188, 189
Till Rehwaldt, Steffen

Giersch: pp. 99, 100, 101
Sami Rintala: pp. 254, 255
Eva Serrats, Jordi Puig: pp. 29, 30, 31, 73, 74-75, 76-77
Joel Sternfeld © 2000: p. 173 (bottom)
thomasmayerarchive.de: pp. 82-83
Steven Turner: p. 211
What if: projects Ltd.: pp. 252, 253
DI Iñaki Zoilo: pp. 60-61
Stiftung Zollverein: p. 80
Gianni Zotta: pp. 230-231